AIR FRYING BAKING CAKES COO

Delicious and Easy Recipes to Follow for Sweet Treats, Pastries, Cakes, and More!

ELENA .D. HARDY

INTRODUCTION

At first glance, the idea of baking cakes in an air fryer may seem a bit strange. Traditional ovens have long been the go-to appliance for baking delicious cakes. However, air fryers have emerged as a versatile cooking tool capable of much more than just frying foods. With their compact size, efficient air circulation, and easy temperature control, air fryers can produce delightfully moist cakes with a perfect rise and delicate crumb.

I'll admit, when I first heard about using an air fryer for baking cakes, I was quite skeptical. How could this small countertop appliance, designed for crispy fried foods, possibly bake a tender, fluffy cake? But after much experimentation and tweaking of recipes, I've become a true believer in the magic of air fryer cake baking.

While baking cakes in an air fryer requires some adjustments to traditional recipes and techniques, the results can be truly impressive. Air fryer cakes often have a superior texture, with a light and airy interior and a beautifully browned exterior. The air fryer's rapid air circulation ensures even baking, eliminating the need to rotate pans or worry about hot spots in the oven. Plus, the compact size of an air fryer means you can enjoy freshly baked treats without heating up a large oven, making it an energy-efficient choice.

One of the things I love most about air fryer cake baking is the level of precision you can achieve. Air fryers allow for incredibly accurate temperature control, often with increments of just a few degrees. This level of precision ensures that your cakes bake evenly and consistently every time, giving you bakery-worthy results right at home.

In this book, I'll guide you through the process of air fryer cake baking, from selecting the right air fryer to mastering techniques for consistently delicious results. We'll explore a variety of cake flavors and styles, each tailored for optimal results in your air fryer. Whether you're a seasoned baker or a novice looking to expand your skills, this guide will provide you with the knowledge and confidence to create impressive cakes with ease.

I remember the first time I pulled a perfectly baked cake out of my air fryer, with a golden-brown crust and a light, fluffy interior. The aroma of fresh-baked cake filled my kitchen, and I couldn't wait to slice into it. That first bite was a revelation – the texture was impeccable, and the flavor was out of this world. From that moment on, I was hooked on the convenience and effectiveness of air fryer baking.

So let's dive in and explore the wonderful world of air fryer cake baking together! Get ready to impress your family and friends with beautiful, delicious cakes that will have them questioning whether they really came from that little air fryer on your countertop.

Overview of Air Fryer Baking for Cakes

At first glance, the idea of baking cakes in an air fryer may seem a bit strange. Traditional ovens have long been the go-to appliance for baking delicious cakes. However, air fryers have emerged as a versatile cooking tool capable of much more than just frying foods. With their compact size, efficient air circulation, and easy temperature control, air fryers can produce delightfully moist cakes with a perfect rise and delicate crumb.

When I first started experimenting with air fryer cake baking, I have to admit, I was a bit of a skeptic. How could this small countertop appliance possibly recreate the environment needed to bake a light, fluffy cake? But after many trials (and perhaps a few failed attempts), I quickly became a believer in the unique capabilities of the air fryer for baking.

While baking cakes in an air fryer requires some adjustments to traditional recipes and techniques, the results can be truly impressive. Air fryer cakes often have a superior texture, with a light and airy interior and a beautifully browned exterior. The rapid air circulation ensures even baking, eliminating the need to rotate pans or worry about hot spots that can plague traditional ovens.

One aspect that really stands out with air fryer cake baking is the level of control you have over the baking environment. Air fryers allow for precise temperature adjustments, often in increments of just a few degrees. This granular temperature control, combined with the efficient air flow, results in incredibly consistent and even baking every single time.

I remember the first time I pulled a perfectly domed vanilla cake out of my air fryer – I was amazed at how flawless it looked. The top had a lovely golden -brown hue, and the sides were straight and smooth. When I sliced into it, I was greeted with a tender, feathery crumb and a melt-in-your-mouth texture. That first bite was absolute perfection, and I knew right then that air fryer cake baking was something special.

Another major benefit of using an air fryer for baking cakes is the compact size and energy efficiency. You can enjoy fresh, homemade cakes without having to heat up a large oven, saving energy and keeping your kitchen cooler. This makes air fryer baking an excellent choice for small spaces like apartments, dorms, or RVs where a full-size oven might not be available.

As you explore the world of air fryer cake baking, you'll find that the possibilities are nearly endless. From classic flavors like moist chocolate cake or zesty lemon Bundt cake, to fun and creative flavor combinations, your air fryer can become a tiny bakery right on your countertop. And with the easy cleanup and virtually no preheating required, whipping up a sweet treat is more convenient than ever before.

So don't be deterred by the unconventional idea of baking cakes in an air fryer. With a bit of guidance and some simple technique adjustments, you'll be churning out professional-quality cakes in no time. Get ready to impress your friends and family with your air fryer baking skills – their jaws will drop when you reveal that those delectable cakes came from that magical little appliance. The world of air fryer desserts awaits!

Benefits of Using an Air Fryer for Baking Cakes

Using an air fryer for baking cakes offers several advantages that make it a worthwhile addition to any baker's arsenal. I first discovered these benefits myself when I started experimenting with air frying cakes out of sheer curiosity. Once I tasted that first perfect air fryer cake, I was hooked and gained a new appreciation for this versatile little appliance.

1. Energy Efficiency: One of the most obvious benefits of air fryer baking is just how energy-efficient it is compared to firing up a full-size conventional oven. Air fryers require less preheating time and consume far less electricity during the actual baking process. This makes them an eco-friendly and cost-effective choice, especially for smaller baking projects. I remember being amazed at how little time it took my air fryer to reach the proper baking temperature, ready to go in just a few minutes.

2. Compact Size: With their compact, countertop-friendly design, air fryers are absolutely ideal for small kitchens, apartments, dorm rooms, or any space-constrained living area. You can easily enjoy freshly baked cakes without the need for a large built-in oven. This has been a game-changer for me in my cozy apartment kitchen with limited counter space.

3. Precise Temperature Control: Have you ever struggled with hot spots or uneven baking in your regular oven? Air fryers allow for incredibly precise temperature control, often with adjustable increments of just a few degrees. This level of precision ensures that your cakes bake evenly and consistently every single time. No more burnt edges or raw centers!

4. Faster Baking Times: Due to the efficient air circulation and heat distribution of air fryers, along with their compact size, baking times are often reduced compared to traditional ovens. This means you can enjoy freshly baked cakes in less time without sacrificing quality. I've had cakes that would normally take an hour to bake come out perfect in 30-40 minutes in my air fryer.

5. Versatility: While air fryers excel at creating crispy fried foods with little oil, their ability to also bake cakes, breads, and other treats adds incredible versatility. With just one compact appliance, you can fry, bake, roast, and more. It's like having an entire oven's worth of functions in one small machine.

I have to admit, when I first started baking with my air fryer, I was a bit nervous about potential pitfalls. Would my cakes rise properly? Would they bake all the way through? Could I really achieve that coveted golden crust? But time after time, my air fryer exceeded my expectations.

One of my favorite examples is a classic yellow birthday cake I made for my nephew's party. I was worried a whole double-layer cake would be too ambitious, but my air fryer handled it like a champ. The layers baked up perfectly level with a tender, delicate crumb. And the icing-like outer crust was pure perfection. My nephew raved about how it was the best birthday cake ever!

From that delicious success, I've continued to be amazed by the capabilities of air fryer cake baking. Decadent chocolate cakes, airy angel food cakes, and even perfectly domed bundt cakes have all come out of my tiny counter-top oven with beautiful and delicious results.

So whether you're a seasoned baker or just starting out, I highly recommend giving air fryer cake baking a try. With its energy efficiency, compact size, temperature precision, quick bake times and versatility, it's a fantastic alternative baking method. Your cakes will come out with bakery-worthy quality, while using a fraction of the energy and space as a traditional oven. Have fun experimenting!

Essential Tools and Ingredients

Before we dive into the techniques of air fryer cake baking, it's important to make sure you have the right tools and ingredients on hand. Having the proper equipment and fresh components will set you up for success right from the start. I've learned this through quite a bit of trial and error in my own air fryer baking adventures!

First and foremost, you'll need an air fryer itself. But not just any air fryer will do if you plan on baking cakes and other desserts. When selecting an air fryer for baking, you'll want to consider the capacity to ensure it can accommodate your desired pan size. Pay close attention to the interior dimensions and keep in mind that cakes will rise up as they bake. An air fryer with a larger basket or tray will give you more flexibility in terms of pan sizes.

You'll also want to make sure your air fryer can reach and maintain the necessary temperatures for baking, which are typically between 300-400°F. Many air fryers top out at 400°F, but some only go as high as 350°F which could limit your baking options. My personal air fryer has a temperature range up to 450°F, giving me nice flexibility.

Once you have your air fryer selected, you'll need some baking pans that can properly fit inside. I prefer using oven-safe pans with removable bottoms, as they allow for easy cake release when it's time to take your baked goodies out. Round or square pans in the 6-8 inch range tend to work best for air fryer baking. Anything much larger may not bake evenly.

Speaking of getting that finished cake out in one piece, it's also wise to invest in some parchment paper liners or quality silicone baking mats. Lining your pans will prevent sticking and make it infinitely easier to remove the delicate cakes after baking. I learned this the hard way with one of my first air fryer cake attempts that completely fell apart as I tried to take it out of the pan!

For mixing up your cake batters, you'll want a nice set of mixing bowls in various sizes. Having multiple bowls allows you to easily separate out dry ingredients from wet. It's also very helpful to have either a hand mixer or a stand mixer on hand for properly aerating the batters. Whipping air into the batter is key for achieving a fluffy, tender crumb on your air fryer cakes.

When it comes to baking ingredients, you'll want to have all the usual suspects like all-purpose flour, granulated and brown sugars, baking powder and baking soda, eggs, milk or buttermilk, oils or melted butter, vanilla extract, and salt. Keeping these basic baking supplies stocked ensures you're always ready to whip up a cake at a moment's notice.

I also recommend having some fun mix-ins and extras on hand to allow you to get creative with your cakes. Things like chocolate chips, sprinkles, fresh or frozen berries, ground spices, citrus zests, and chopped nuts can take a basic cake to new and delicious heights.

Finally, for decorating your air-fried cakes into showstoppers, you'll want to have some essential tools like an offset spatula for icing, piping bags and tips for detail work, a turntable for easy frosting, and decorations like sprinkles or candies.

With the right air fryer, bakeware, mixing tools, fresh ingredients, and decorating supplies, you'll be all set to dive into the wonderful world of air fryer cake baking. Having everything prepped and ready to go means you're just a few steps away from impressing your friends and family with professional-quality baked treats. Let's get baking!

CHAPTER ONE: GETTING STARTED WITH YOUR AIR FRYER

Now that you've gathered all the essential tools and ingredients for air fryer cake baking, it's time to get familiar with your new compact oven. While air fryers are incredibly user-friendly, there are a few tips and tricks that will help ensure consistent, delicious results every time you bake.

Choosing the Right Air Fryer

If you haven't purchased an air fryer yet, this first step is crucial. With so many models on the market, it can feel overwhelming trying to pick the right one. My advice? Pay close attention to the capacity, temperature range, controls, and any additional features.

Capacity is one of the biggest factors when selecting an air fryer for baking. You'll want an interior space large enough to comfortably fit your desired cake pans while still allowing room for air to properly circulate around them. Shooting for at least a 5- or 6-quart basket size gives you nice flexibility. Any smaller and you'll be quite limited in which cakes you can make. Larger models around 8 quarts open up possibilities for bigger Bundt cakes or layered creations.

However, you don't necessarily want to go too big either, as an excessive amount of interior space can make it harder to maintain consistent, even heat distribution. I found this out the hard way when I initially purchased an air fryer oven with multiple racks thinking I could bake multiple cakes at once. While achievable with careful temperature and positioning adjustments, it introduced a lot more room for error compared to the more compact air fryers.

Temperature range is another crucial specification. At a minimum, you'll want an air fryer that can reach at least 350°F, but ideally look for models that go up to 400°F or higher. This broad range allows you to properly bake everything from light cakes and breads to richer, denser treats. Some units even have a specific "Bake" function programmed in for hassle-free air frying baked goods.

I remember one of my early air fryer models could only reach 370°F as its maximum temperature. While I could achieve decent results for simple cakes, I really struggled with recipes that required higher heat for proper rise and browning. Once I upgraded to an air fryer oven that topped out at 450°F, I had infinitely more options and much better success.

The control panel is another factor to consider when choosing an air fryer for baking. Look for models with intuitive digital controls that allow you to easily adjust the temperature in small 5°F or less increments. Being able to set the air fryer to the perfect degree makes a big difference in perfecting recipes. Some budget models only give you a handful of preset temperature options which really limits your flexibility.

You'll also want controls that allow you to set an audible timer, letting you know exactly when to check your cakes instead of having to keep peeking in the window or lifting the basket. Units with built-in temperature probes can be great for taking any guesswork out of doneness too.

While not a must-haves, some additional features can come in handy specifically for baking. Models with an internal light help you monitor browning without disrupting the air flow. Rotating baskets or synchronized air flow can improve overall heat circulation. And pre-programmed convection or baking modes automatically adjust times and temperatures for you.

But don't get too caught up prioritizing fancy extras over the core capacity, temperature range, and control capabilities. You can bake delicious cakes in a simple, budget-friendly model as long as it has those critical baking functions covered.

Preheating Techniques

Once you've got the perfect air fryer selected, the next step is to master preheating. Proper preheating ensures even heat distribution from the start for beautifully consistent results.

Unlike traditional ovens that can take 30 minutes or more to fully preheat, air fryers typically only need between 5-10 minutes thanks to their compact size and high efficiency heating elements. But you'll still want to preheat each and every time rather than trying to speed things up by skipping this crucial step.

Always refer to your specific air fryer model's instructions for proper preheating times. As a general rule, smaller 3–4-quart units heat up a bit quicker than larger capacities in the 5–7-quart range. But don't try to rush it by setting a higher temperature initially then reducing once preheated. Allow the air fryer to steadily reach and stabilize at the intended baking temperature from the start.

During the preheating cycle, I highly recommend placing an oven-safe pan, dish, or baking tray into the air fryer basket. This "hot surface" serves two important purposes. First, it helps absorb and distribute the heat more evenly so there are no hot or cold spots surrounding your cake pan. Secondly, having a preheated solid surface prevents soggy bottoms by instantly starting a light crust on the batter as soon as you add it in later.

I learned this preheat pan trick the hard way with one of my early lemon bundt cake experiments. I simply sprayed the air fryer basket and added in the batter without any extra pan. While the outer shape baked up nicely browned and domed, the bottom remained pale, dense, and underwhelmed in both flavor and texture. Preheating a dark baking pan along with the air fryer resolved that issue perfectly!

If your air fryer model doesn't include an internal temperature probe, I also recommend using a small oven thermometer to verify it has reached your desired temperature before adding in your cake batter. These inexpensive thermometers can confirm if your machine is running a little hot or cold compared to the displayed temp.

Be sure to allow the air fryer to fully complete the preheat cycle before opening to add in your cake pan. Repeatedly opening and closing the basket during preheating can cause heat loss and uneven temperatures. Have your prepared batter and pan ready to go as soon as that preheat notification sounds.

Tips for Adapting Traditional Cake Recipes

Part of the fun of air fryer baking is being able to take your existing favorite cake recipes and give them a whirl in this unconventional little oven. With some simple modifications, you can transform treasured family desserts or blogger hits into perfectly portioned air fryer creations.

The very first adjustment I always make when converting traditional recipes is reducing the oven temperature by 25°F. Air fryers run incredibly hot compared to normal ovens because of that intense air circulation in the compact chamber. Baking at the full oven temp listed often leads to over-browning on the outer layers before the interior has finished cooking through.

For example, let's say a recipe calls for baking at 350°F. For the air fryer version, I'll set the temperature to 325°F instead. This 25-degree reduction allows for more gradual and even baking without risk of burning before the center sets up.

You'll also need to adjust the baking time, but it's difficult to give an exact conversion rate since air fryers can vary quite a bit between models and sizes. My general rule of thumb is to start checking for doneness about 5-10 minutes earlier than the original recipe's recommended time. Use the tried-and-true toothpick or skewer test, inserting it into the deepest part of the cake. If it comes out cleanly without any wet batter, your cake is likely done!

If the toothpick shows unbaked batter after your initial time check, no need to panic. Simply return the cake to the air fryer and check again in 5-minute increments until a toothpick finally comes out with just a few crumbs clinging to it. Make a note of the total time needed for that particular recipe so you'll know for next time.

One other major change you'll likely need to make is using smaller cake pans to accommodate the air fryer's compact interior space. While you can occasionally find air fryer models large enough for a full 9-inch round, most require scaling down to 6 or 8-inch pans instead.

If you have your heart set on making a larger tiered cake, I suggest splitting the batter between two or three of those smaller 6 or 8-inch pans to bake in batches. Then you can torte and stack them with frosting or filling once they've all cooled. It's a bit more work upfront, but the payoff of a towering showpiece cake is worth the extra effort!

No matter what pan size you use, it's absolutely critical to take proper precautions against sticking. Generously grease the entire pan, line with parchment rounds or silicone baking mats, and avoid using old pans with build-up and scratches. The efficient air frying process combined with sugar from batters creates the perfect storm for baked goods to adhere stubbornly to any imperfect surfaces.

I still vividly remember the utter despair of watching a beautiful dark chocolate bundt cake slowly crumble and break apart as I tried removing it from an improperly greased pan. What should have been a rich, celebratory dessert ended up a pile of rubble despite my best efforts at coaxing it out in one piece. Lesson learned - take the time to thoroughly prep your pans!

Finally, take care to watch for any potential batter overflow as your cakes rise up in the air fryer. Halfway through baking, I'll often take a peek through the window and tent the top loosely with a strip of foil if it's getting overly browned or puffed up. Foil tents deflect some of that intense heating element while still allowing air flow.

With these simple tips for choosing the ideal air fryer, mastering preheating, and making recipe adjustments, you'll have all the groundwork laid for showstopping desserts. The magic of bakery-level air fryer cakes awaits!

CHAPTER TWO: CLASSIC CAKE RECIPES

Perfect Victoria Sponge Cake

Prep: 15 mins | Cook: 25 mins | Serves: 8 slices

Ingredients:
- 200g (1 cup) caster sugar
- 200g (1 cup) unsalted butter, softened
- 200g (1 ⅔ cups) self-raising flour
- 4 large eggs
- 1 tsp baking powder
- 2 tbsp strawberry jam
- Icing sugar, for dusting

Instructions:
1. Preheat your Air Fryer Baking Cakes to 160°C (320°F).
2. Cream together sugar and butter until light and fluffy.
3. Beat in eggs, one at a time.
4. Sift in flour and baking powder, gently fold until combined.
5. Pour batter into a greased cake tin.
6. Cook in the Air Fryer Baking Cakes for 25 minutes or until a skewer comes out clean.
7. Let cool in the tin for 5 minutes, then transfer to a wire rack.
8. Once cooled, spread jam on one cake layer, top with the other layer, and dust with icing sugar.

Nutritional Info: Calories: 320 | Fat: 15g | Carbs: 42g | Protein: 4g

Air fryer Function used: Bake

Luscious Lemon Drizzle Cake

Prep: 10 mins | Cook: 30 mins | Serves: 8 slices

Ingredients:

- 175g (¾ cup) caster sugar
- 175g (¾ cup) unsalted butter, softened
- 175g (1 ⅓ cups) self-raising flour
- 3 large eggs
- Zest of 2 lemons
- Juice of 1 lemon
- 75g (⅓ cup) granulated sugar

Instructions:

1. Preheat Air Fryer Baking Cakes to 160°C (320°F).
2. Cream together caster sugar and butter until pale and fluffy.
3. Beat in eggs, one at a time, then add lemon zest.
4. Sift in flour and gently fold until smooth.
5. Pour batter into a greased cake tin.
6. Bake in the Air Fryer Baking Cakes for 30 minutes or until golden and firm to touch.
7. Mix lemon juice with granulated sugar.
8. Once the cake is baked, poke holes with a skewer and pour over the lemon-sugar mixture.

Nutritional Info: Calories: 290 | Fat: 14g | Carbs: 38g | Protein: 4g

Air fryer Function used: Bake

Decadent Chocolate Fudge Cake

Prep: 15 mins | Cook: 35 mins | Serves: 8

Ingredients:

- 200g (1 cup) caster sugar
- 150g (1 ¼ cups) all-purpose flour
- 50g (½ cup) cocoa powder
- 1 tsp baking powder
- ½ tsp baking soda
- 2 large eggs
- 120ml (½ cup) milk
- 120ml (½ cup) vegetable oil
- 1 tsp vanilla extract
- 120ml (½ cup) boiling water
- Chocolate frosting, for topping

Instructions:

1. Preheat your Air Fryer to 160°C (320°F).
2. In a large bowl, whisk together the sugar, flour, cocoa powder, baking powder, and baking soda.
3. Add the eggs, milk, vegetable oil, and vanilla extract to the dry ingredients. Mix until well combined.
4. Gradually pour in the boiling water, stirring continuously until the batter is smooth.
5. Pour the batter into a greased and lined cake tin suitable for the Air Fryer.
6. Place the tin in the Air Fryer basket and bake for 30-35 minutes or until a skewer inserted into the center comes out clean.
7. Allow the cake to cool completely before frosting.

Nutritional Info: Calories: 312 | Fat: 15g | Carbs: 43g | Protein: 5g

Air Fryer Function Used: Bake

Air Fryer Carrot Cake

Prep: 20 mins | Cook: 40 mins | Serves: 8

Ingredients:

- 200g (1 cup) light brown sugar
- 150ml (½ cup) vegetable oil
- 3 large eggs
- 200g (1 ½ cups) self-raising flour
- 1 tsp baking powder
- 1 tsp ground cinnamon
- ½ tsp ground nutmeg
- 200g (1 ½ cups) grated carrots
- 75g (½ cup) chopped walnuts (optional)
- Cream cheese frosting, for topping

Instructions:

1. Preheat your Air Fryer to 160°C (320°F).
2. In a large bowl, whisk together the brown sugar and vegetable oil until well combined.
3. Add the eggs one at a time, mixing well after each addition.
4. Sift in the flour, baking powder, cinnamon, and nutmeg. Mix until just combined.
5. Fold in the grated carrots and chopped walnuts, if using.
6. Pour the batter into a greased and lined cake tin suitable for the Air Fryer.
7. Place the tin in the Air Fryer basket and bake for 35-40 minutes or until a skewer inserted into the center comes out clean.
8. Allow the cake to cool completely before frosting with cream cheese frosting.

Nutritional Info: Calories: 297 | Fat: 17g | Carbs: 34g | Protein: 5g

Air Fryer Function Used: Bake

Air Fryer Banana Bread

Prep: 15 mins | Cook: 45 mins | Serves: 8

Ingredients:

- 3 ripe bananas, mashed
- 150g (¾ cup) caster sugar
- 1 large egg, beaten
- 60ml (¼ cup) vegetable oil
- 1 tsp vanilla extract
- 190g (1 ½ cups) all-purpose flour
- 1 tsp baking soda
- Pinch of salt

Instructions:

1. Preheat your Air Fryer to 160°C (320°F).
2. In a mixing bowl, combine the mashed bananas, caster sugar, beaten egg, vegetable oil, and vanilla extract.
3. Sift in the flour, baking soda, and salt. Mix until just combined.
4. Pour the batter into a greased and lined loaf tin that fits in your Air Fryer basket.
5. Place the tin in the Air Fryer basket and bake for 40-45 minutes or until a skewer inserted into the center comes out clean.
6. Allow the banana bread to cool in the tin for 10 minutes before transferring to a wire rack to cool completely.

Nutritional Info: Calories: 241 | Fat: 7g | Carbs: 43g | Protein: 3g

Air Fryer Function Used: Bake

Air Fryer Pineapple Upside-Down Cake

Prep: 20 mins | Cook: 30 mins | Serves: 8

Ingredients:
- 400g (1 ¾ cups) canned pineapple slices, drained
- 50g (¼ cup) unsalted butter, melted
- 100g (½ cup) light brown sugar
- 150g (1 ¼ cups) all-purpose flour
- 1 tsp baking powder
- ½ tsp baking soda
- 100g (½ cup) granulated sugar
- 1 large egg
- 120ml (½ cup) buttermilk
- 60ml (¼ cup) vegetable oil
- 1 tsp vanilla extract
- Maraschino cherries, for garnish (optional)

Instructions:
1. Preheat your Air Fryer to 160°C (320°F).
2. Grease the bottom of your Air Fryer cake pan or a cake tin that fits in the basket with melted butter.
3. Arrange the pineapple slices in the bottom of the pan and sprinkle with light brown sugar.
4. In a mixing bowl, whisk together the flour, baking powder, and baking soda.
5. In another bowl, whisk together the granulated sugar, egg, buttermilk, vegetable oil, and vanilla extract until smooth.
6. Gradually add the wet ingredients to the dry ingredients, mixing until just combined.
7. Pour the batter over the pineapple slices in the pan.
8. Place the pan in the Air Fryer basket and bake for 25-30 minutes or until a skewer inserted into the center comes out clean.
9. Allow the cake to cool for 5 minutes, then invert it onto a serving plate. Garnish with maraschino cherries if desired.

Nutritional Info: Calories: 287 | Fat: 11g | Carbs: 45g | Protein: 4g

Air Fryer Function Used: Bake

Air Fryer Red Velvet Cake

Prep: 15 mins | Cook: 30 mins | Serves: 8

Ingredients:
- 200g (1 cup) caster sugar
- 120ml (½ cup) vegetable oil
- 2 large eggs
- 1 tbsp cocoa powder
- 1 tsp vanilla extract
- ½ tsp red food coloring
- 200g (1 ¼ cups) all-purpose flour
- ½ tsp baking soda
- 120ml (½ cup) buttermilk
- 1 tsp white vinegar
- Cream cheese frosting, for topping

Instructions:
1. Preheat your Air Fryer to 160°C (320°F).
2. In a large bowl, whisk together the caster sugar and vegetable oil until well combined.
3. Beat in the eggs, one at a time, then stir in the cocoa powder, vanilla extract, and red food coloring.
4. Sift in the flour and baking soda, then fold in the buttermilk and white vinegar until just combined.
5. Pour the batter into a greased and lined cake tin suitable for the Air Fryer.
6. Place the tin in the Air Fryer basket and bake for 25-30 minutes or until a skewer inserted into the center comes out clean.
7. Allow the cake to cool completely before frosting with cream cheese frosting.

Nutritional Info: Calories: 309 | Fat: 15g | Carbs: 41g | Protein: 4g

Air Fryer Function Used: Bake

Air Fryer Blueberry Buckle

Prep: 15 mins | Cook: 35 mins | Serves: 8

Ingredients:

- 150g (1 ¼ cups) all-purpose flour
- 1 tsp baking powder
- ¼ tsp salt
- 60g (¼ cup) unsalted butter, softened
- 100g (½ cup) granulated sugar
- 1 large egg
- 60ml (¼ cup) milk
- 1 tsp vanilla extract
- 150g (1 cup) fresh blueberries
- Streusel topping:
- 50g (¼ cup) granulated sugar
- 35g (¼ cup) all-purpose flour
- ½ tsp ground cinnamon
- 30g (2 tbsp) unsalted butter, melted

Instructions:

1. Preheat your Air Fryer to 160°C (320°F).
2. Grease a cake tin suitable for the Air Fryer.
3. In a small bowl, combine the streusel topping ingredients: sugar, flour, cinnamon, and melted butter. Mix until crumbly and set aside.
4. In a medium bowl, whisk together the flour, baking powder, and salt.
5. In a separate bowl, cream together the softened butter and sugar until light and fluffy.
6. Beat in the egg, milk, and vanilla extract until well combined.
7. Gradually add the dry ingredients to the wet ingredients, mixing until just combined.
8. Gently fold in the fresh blueberries.
9. Pour the batter into the greased cake tin and spread it out evenly.
10. Sprinkle the streusel topping over the batter.
11. Place the tin in the Air Fryer basket and bake for 30-35 minutes or until a skewer inserted into the center comes out clean.
12. Allow the buckle to cool slightly before serving.

Nutritional Info: Calories: 242 | Fat: 9g | Carbs: 38g | Protein: 3g

Air Fryer Function Used: Bake

Air Fryer Strawberry Shortcake

Prep: 20 mins | Cook: 25 mins | Serves: 6

Ingredients:

- 200g (1 ¾ cups) all-purpose flour
- 50g (¼ cup) granulated sugar
- 1 tbsp baking powder
- ½ tsp salt
- 85g (6 tbsp) unsalted butter, cold and cubed
- 120ml (½ cup) milk
- 1 tsp vanilla extract
- 300g (2 cups) fresh strawberries, sliced
- Whipped cream, for topping

Instructions:

1. Preheat your Air Fryer to 160°C (320°F).
2. In a large bowl, whisk together the flour, sugar, baking powder, and salt.
3. Add the cold cubed butter to the flour mixture and use your fingertips to rub it in until the mixture resembles coarse breadcrumbs.
4. Stir in the milk and vanilla extract until the dough comes together.
5. Turn the dough out onto a floured surface and gently knead it a few times until smooth.
6. Roll out the dough to about 1-inch thickness and use a round cutter to cut out biscuits.
7. Place the biscuits in the Air Fryer basket, leaving a little space between each one.
8. Bake for 20-25 minutes or until the biscuits are golden brown and cooked through.
9. Allow the biscuits to cool slightly, then split them in half.
10. Top each biscuit with sliced strawberries and whipped cream before serving.

Nutritional Info: Calories: 278 | Fat: 11g | Carbs: 41g | Protein: 4g

Air Fryer Function Used: Bake

Air Fryer Apple Cake

Prep: 20 mins | Cook: 35 mins | Serves: 8

Ingredients:

- 3 large apples, peeled, cored, and diced
- 200g (1 cup) granulated sugar
- 2 large eggs
- 120ml (½ cup) vegetable oil
- 1 tsp vanilla extract
- 200g (1 ½ cups) all-purpose flour
- 1 tsp baking powder
- ½ tsp baking soda
- 1 tsp ground cinnamon
- ¼ tsp salt
- Powdered sugar, for dusting

Instructions:

1. Preheat your Air Fryer to 160°C (320°F).
2. In a large bowl, mix together the diced apples and granulated sugar. Let them sit for 10 minutes to release their juices.
3. After 10 minutes, beat in the eggs, vegetable oil, and vanilla extract until well combined.
4. In another bowl, sift together the flour, baking powder, baking soda, cinnamon, and salt.
5. Gradually add the dry ingredients to the wet ingredients, mixing until just combined.
6. Pour the batter into a greased and lined cake tin suitable for the Air Fryer.
7. Place the tin in the Air Fryer basket and bake for 30-35 minutes or until a skewer inserted into the center comes out clean.
8. Allow the cake to cool slightly before dusting with powdered sugar.

Nutritional Info: Calories: 298 | Fat: 12g | Carbs: 45g | Protein: 4g

Air Fryer Function Used: Bake

Air Fryer Coconut Cake

Prep: 15 mins | Cook: 30 mins | Serves: 8

Ingredients:

- 200g (1 cup) caster sugar
- 3 large eggs
- 120ml (½ cup) coconut milk
- 60ml (¼ cup) vegetable oil
- 1 tsp vanilla extract
- 200g (1 ½ cups) all-purpose flour
- 2 tsp baking powder
- ¼ tsp salt
- 100g (1 cup) shredded coconut
- Coconut frosting, for topping

Instructions:

1. Preheat your Air Fryer to 160°C (320°F).
2. In a mixing bowl, whisk together the caster sugar, eggs, coconut milk, vegetable oil, and vanilla extract until well combined.
3. In another bowl, sift together the flour, baking powder, and salt.
4. Gradually add the dry ingredients to the wet ingredients, mixing until just combined.
5. Fold in the shredded coconut.
6. Pour the batter into a greased and lined cake tin suitable for the Air Fryer.
7. Place the tin in the Air Fryer basket and bake for 25-30 minutes or until a skewer inserted into the center comes out clean.
8. Allow the cake to cool completely before frosting with coconut frosting.

Nutritional Info: Calories: 315 | Fat: 14g | Carbs: 42g | Protein: 5g

Air Fryer Function Used: Bake

Air Fryer Gingerbread Cake

Prep: 20 mins | Cook: 30 mins | Serves: 8

Ingredients:

- 200g (1 cup) molasses
- 120ml (½ cup) boiling water
- 120g (½ cup) unsalted butter, melted
- 150g (¾ cup) brown sugar
- 2 large eggs
- 280g (2 ¼ cups) all-purpose flour
- 1 ½ tsp baking soda
- 1 tsp ground ginger
- 1 tsp ground cinnamon
- ¼ tsp ground cloves
- ¼ tsp salt
- Powdered sugar, for dusting

Instructions:

1. Preheat your Air Fryer to 160°C (320°F).
2. In a large mixing bowl, combine the molasses and boiling water.
3. Stir in the melted butter and brown sugar until dissolved.
4. Beat in the eggs one at a time until well incorporated.
5. In a separate bowl, sift together the flour, baking soda, ginger, cinnamon, cloves, and salt.
6. Gradually add the dry ingredients to the wet ingredients, mixing until just combined.
7. Pour the batter into a greased and lined cake tin suitable for the Air Fryer.
8. Place the tin in the Air Fryer basket and bake for 25-30 minutes or until a skewer inserted into the center comes out clean.
9. Allow the cake to cool slightly before dusting with powdered sugar.

Nutritional Info: Calories: 302 | Fat: 10g | Carbs: 49g | Protein: 4g

Air Fryer Function Used: Bake

Air Fryer Marble Cake

Prep: 15 mins | Cook: 30 mins | Serves: 8

Ingredients:

- 200g (1 cup) granulated sugar
- 120g (½ cup) unsalted butter, softened
- 3 large eggs
- 180ml (¾ cup) milk
- 1 tsp vanilla extract
- 200g (1 ½ cups) all-purpose flour
- 2 tsp baking powder
- 2 tbsp cocoa powder
- Powdered sugar, for dusting

Instructions:

1. Preheat your Air Fryer to 160°C (320°F).
2. In a mixing bowl, cream together the granulated sugar and softened butter until light and fluffy.
3. Beat in the eggs one at a time, then stir in the milk and vanilla extract.
4. Sift in the flour and baking powder, mixing until smooth.
5. Divide the batter evenly into two bowls.
6. In one bowl, fold in the cocoa powder until fully incorporated.
7. Spoon alternate dollops of the vanilla and chocolate batters into a greased and lined cake tin suitable for the Air Fryer.
8. Use a skewer or knife to gently swirl the batters together to create a marbled effect.
9. Place the tin in the Air Fryer basket and bake for 25-30 minutes or until a skewer inserted into the center comes out clean.
10. Allow the cake to cool slightly before dusting with powdered sugar.

Nutritional Info: Calories: 272 | Fat: 11g | Carbs: 39g | Protein: 4g

Air Fryer Function Used: Bake

Air Fryer Hummingbird Cake

Prep: 20 mins | Cook: 35 mins | Serves: 8

Ingredients:
- 200g (1 cup) granulated sugar
- 150ml (⅔ cup) vegetable oil
- 2 large eggs
- 1 tsp vanilla extract
- 200g (1 ½ cups) all-purpose flour
- 1 tsp baking soda
- ½ tsp ground cinnamon
- ½ tsp ground nutmeg
- 200g (1 cup) mashed ripe bananas
- 100g (½ cup) crushed pineapple, drained
- 75g (½ cup) chopped pecans
- Cream cheese frosting, for topping

Instructions:
1. Preheat your Air Fryer to 160°C (320°F).
2. In a large bowl, whisk together the granulated sugar, vegetable oil, eggs, and vanilla extract until well combined.
3. In another bowl, sift together the flour, baking soda, cinnamon, and nutmeg.
4. Gradually add the dry ingredients to the wet ingredients, mixing until just combined.
5. Fold in the mashed bananas, crushed pineapple, and chopped pecans.
6. Pour the batter into a greased and lined cake tin suitable for the Air Fryer.
7. Place the tin in the Air Fryer basket and bake for 30-35 minutes or until a skewer inserted into the center comes out clean.
8. Allow the cake to cool completely before frosting with cream cheese frosting.

Nutritional Info: Calories: 358 | Fat: 20g | Carbs: 41g | Protein: 4g

Air Fryer Function Used: Bake

Air Fryer Spiced Pumpkin Cake

Prep: 20 mins | Cook: 40 mins | Serves: 8

Ingredients:
- 200g (1 cup) granulated sugar
- 120ml (½ cup) vegetable oil
- 2 large eggs
- 200g (1 ½ cups) all-purpose flour
- 1 tsp baking powder
- ½ tsp baking soda
- ½ tsp salt
- 1 tsp ground cinnamon
- ½ tsp ground nutmeg
- ½ tsp ground ginger
- 200g (1 cup) canned pumpkin puree
- Cream cheese frosting, for topping

Instructions:
1. Preheat your Air Fryer to 160°C (320°F).
2. In a large bowl, whisk together the granulated sugar, vegetable oil, and eggs until well combined.
3. In another bowl, sift together the flour, baking powder, baking soda, salt, cinnamon, nutmeg, and ginger.
4. Gradually add the dry ingredients to the wet ingredients, mixing until just combined.
5. Fold in the canned pumpkin puree until evenly distributed.
6. Pour the batter into a greased and lined cake tin suitable for the Air Fryer.
7. Place the tin in the Air Fryer basket and bake for 35-40 minutes or until a skewer inserted into the center comes out clean.
8. Allow the cake to cool completely before frosting with cream cheese frosting.

Nutritional Info: Calories: 315 | Fat: 17g | Carbs: 38g | Protein: 4g

Air Fryer Function Used: Bake

Air Fryer Lemon Pound Cake

Prep: 15 mins | Cook: 35 mins | Serves: 8

Ingredients:

- 200g (1 cup) unsalted butter, softened
- 200g (1 cup) granulated sugar
- 4 large eggs
- 1 tsp vanilla extract
- Zest of 2 lemons
- 240g (2 cups) all-purpose flour
- 1 tsp baking powder
- ½ tsp salt
- 60ml (¼ cup) lemon juice
- Powdered sugar, for dusting

Instructions:

1. Preheat your Air Fryer to 160°C (320°F).
2. In a large mixing bowl, cream together the softened butter and granulated sugar until light and fluffy.
3. Beat in the eggs, one at a time, then stir in the vanilla extract and lemon zest.
4. In another bowl, sift together the flour, baking powder, and salt.
5. Gradually add the dry ingredients to the wet ingredients, mixing until just combined.
6. Stir in the lemon juice until evenly distributed.
7. Pour the batter into a greased and lined cake tin suitable for the Air Fryer.
8. Place the tin in the Air Fryer basket and bake for 30-35 minutes or until a skewer inserted into the center comes out clean.
9. Allow the cake to cool slightly before dusting with powdered sugar.

Nutritional Info: Calories: 337 | Fat: 17g | Carbs: 42g | Protein: 5g

Air Fryer Function Used: Bake

CHAPTER THREE: CUPCAKE AND MUFFIN DELIGHTS

Air Fryer Vanilla Cupcakes

Prep: 15 mins | Cook: 15 mins | Serves: 12 cupcakes

Ingredients:
- 150g (1 ¼ cups) all-purpose flour
- 1 ½ tsp baking powder
- ¼ tsp salt
- 115g (½ cup) unsalted butter, softened
- 150g (¾ cup) caster sugar
- 2 large eggs
- 1 tsp vanilla extract
- 120ml (½ cup) milk

Instructions:
1. Preheat your Air Fryer to 160°C (320°F) for 5 minutes.
2. In a bowl, whisk together flour, baking powder, and salt.
3. In another bowl, beat softened butter and caster sugar until creamy.
4. Add eggs, one at a time, and beat well after each addition. Mix in vanilla extract.
5. Gradually add the dry ingredients and milk to the wet mixture, alternating between the two, beginning and ending with the dry ingredients.
6. Line cupcake molds with liners and fill each about 2/3 full with batter.
7. Place the cupcake molds in the Air Fryer basket, ensuring space between each mold for air circulation.
8. Air fry at 160°C (320°F) for 12-15 minutes or until a toothpick inserted into the center comes out clean.
9. Once done, remove cupcakes from the Air Fryer and let them cool completely before frosting.

Nutritional Info: Calories: 180 | Fat: 8g | Carbs: 24g | Protein: 3g

Air Fryer Function Used: Bake

Air Fryer Chocolate Cupcakes

Prep: 15 mins | Cook: 15 mins | Serves: 12 cupcakes

Ingredients:
- 140g (1 cup) all-purpose flour
- 40g (½ cup) unsweetened cocoa powder
- 1 tsp baking powder
- ½ tsp baking soda
- ¼ tsp salt
- 100g (½ cup) caster sugar
- 100g (½ cup) brown sugar
- 2 large eggs
- 120ml (½ cup) milk
- 60ml (¼ cup) vegetable oil
- 1 tsp vanilla extract
- 120ml (½ cup) boiling water

Instructions:
1. Preheat your Air Fryer to 160°C (320°F) for 5 minutes.
2. In a bowl, sift together flour, cocoa powder, baking powder, baking soda, and salt.
3. In another bowl, whisk together caster sugar, brown sugar, eggs, milk, vegetable oil, and vanilla extract until smooth.
4. Gradually add the dry ingredients to the wet mixture, stirring until just combined.
5. Pour in boiling water and mix until smooth.
6. Line cupcake molds with liners and fill each about 2/3 full with batter.
7. Place the cupcake molds in the Air Fryer basket, ensuring space between each mold for air circulation.
8. Air fry at 160°C (320°F) for 12-15 minutes or until a toothpick inserted into the center comes out clean.
9. Once done, remove cupcakes from the Air Fryer and let them cool completely before frosting.

Nutritional Info: Calories: 210 | Fat: 9g | Carbs: 31g | Protein: 3g

Air Fryer Function Used: Bake

Air Fryer Lemon Cupcakes

Prep: 15 mins | Cook: 15 mins | Serves: 12 cupcakes

Ingredients:
- 150g (1 ¼ cups) all-purpose flour
- 1 ½ tsp baking powder
- ¼ tsp salt
- 115g (½ cup) unsalted butter, softened
- 150g (¾ cup) caster sugar
- 2 large eggs
- Zest of 1 lemon
- 2 tbsp lemon juice
- 120ml (½ cup) milk
- Lemon frosting, for topping

Instructions:
1. Preheat your Air Fryer to 160°C (320°F) for 5 minutes.
2. In a bowl, whisk together flour, baking powder, and salt.
3. In another bowl, beat softened butter and caster sugar until creamy.
4. Add eggs, one at a time, and beat well after each addition. Mix in lemon zest and juice.
5. Gradually add the dry ingredients and milk to the wet mixture, alternating between the two, beginning and ending with the dry ingredients.
6. Line cupcake molds with liners and fill each about 2/3 full with batter.
7. Place the cupcake molds in the Air Fryer basket, ensuring space between each mold for air circulation.
8. Air fry at 160°C (320°F) for 12-15 minutes or until a toothpick inserted into the center comes out clean.
9. Once done, remove cupcakes from the Air Fryer and let them cool completely before frosting with lemon frosting.

Nutritional Info: Calories: 190 | Fat: 8g | Carbs: 27g | Protein: 3g

Air Fryer Function Used: Bake

Air Fryer Red Velvet Cupcakes

Prep: 15 mins | Cook: 15 mins | Serves: 12 cupcakes

Ingredients:

- 150g (1 ¼ cups) all-purpose flour
- 1 tbsp unsweetened cocoa powder
- ½ tsp baking soda
- ¼ tsp salt
- 115g (½ cup) unsalted butter, softened
- 150g (¾ cup) caster sugar
- 2 large eggs
- 1 tsp vanilla extract
- 1 tsp white vinegar
- 1 tsp red food coloring
- 120ml (½ cup) buttermilk
- Cream cheese frosting, for topping

Instructions:

1. Preheat your Air Fryer to 160°C (320°F) for 5 minutes.
2. In a bowl, sift together flour, cocoa powder, baking soda, and salt.
3. In another bowl, beat softened butter and caster sugar until creamy.
4. Add eggs, one at a time, and beat well after each addition. Mix in vanilla extract, white vinegar, and red food coloring.
5. Gradually add the dry ingredients and buttermilk to the wet mixture, alternating between the two, beginning and ending with the dry ingredients.
6. Line cupcake molds with liners and fill each about 2/3 full with batter.
7. Place the cupcake molds in the Air Fryer basket, ensuring space between each mold for air circulation.
8. Air fry at 160°C (320°F) for 12-15 minutes or until a toothpick inserted into the center comes out clean.
9. Once done, remove cupcakes from the Air Fryer and let them cool completely before frosting with cream cheese frosting.

Nutritional Info: Calories: 200 | Fat: 9g | Carbs: 27g | Protein: 3g

Air Fryer Function Used: Bake

Air Fryer Blueberry Muffins

Prep: 15 mins | Cook: 20 mins | Serves: 12 muffins

Ingredients:
- 250g (2 cups) all-purpose flour
- 150g (¾ cup) granulated sugar
- 2 tsp baking powder
- ¼ tsp salt
- 2 large eggs
- 120ml (½ cup) milk
- 120ml (½ cup) vegetable oil
- 1 tsp vanilla extract
- 200g (1 ½ cups) fresh blueberries

Instructions:
1. Preheat your Air Fryer to 160°C (320°F) for 5 minutes.
2. In a large bowl, whisk together flour, sugar, baking powder, and salt.
3. In another bowl, beat eggs, then stir in milk, vegetable oil, and vanilla extract.
4. Pour the wet ingredients into the dry ingredients and mix until just combined.
5. Gently fold in the blueberries.
6. Line muffin cups with paper liners and fill each about 2/3 full with batter.
7. Place the muffin cups in the Air Fryer basket, ensuring space between each muffin for air circulation.
8. Air fry at 160°C (320°F) for 18-20 minutes or until a toothpick inserted into the center comes out clean.
9. Once done, remove muffins from the Air Fryer and let them cool slightly before serving.

Nutritional Info: Calories: 210 | Fat: 10g | Carbs: 27g | Protein: 3g

Air Fryer Function Used: Bake

Air Fryer Banana Muffins

Prep: 15 mins | Cook: 20 mins | Serves: 12 muffins

Ingredients:
- 3 ripe bananas, mashed
- 150g (¾ cup) granulated sugar
- 1 large egg
- 60ml (¼ cup) unsalted butter, melted
- 120ml (½ cup) milk
- 1 tsp vanilla extract
- 250g (2 cups) all-purpose flour
- 1 tsp baking powder
- ½ tsp baking soda
- ¼ tsp salt

Instructions:
1. Preheat your Air Fryer to 160°C (320°F) for 5 minutes.
2. In a large bowl, mix mashed bananas, sugar, egg, melted butter, milk, and vanilla extract until well combined.
3. In another bowl, sift together flour, baking powder, baking soda, and salt.
4. Gradually add the dry ingredients to the wet ingredients, stirring until just combined.
5. Line muffin cups with paper liners and fill each about 2/3 full with batter.
6. Place the muffin cups in the Air Fryer basket, ensuring space between each muffin for air circulation.
7. Air fry at 160°C (320°F) for 18-20 minutes or until a toothpick inserted into the center comes out clean.
8. Once done, remove muffins from the Air Fryer and let them cool slightly before serving.

Nutritional Info:

Air Fryer Chocolate Chip Muffins

Prep: 15 mins | Cook: 20 mins | Serves: 12 muffins

Ingredients:
- 250g (2 cups) all-purpose flour
- 100g (½ cup) granulated sugar
- 2 tsp baking powder
- ¼ tsp salt
- 1 large egg
- 120ml (½ cup) milk
- 120ml (½ cup) vegetable oil
- 1 tsp vanilla extract
- 100g (¾ cup) chocolate chips

Instructions:
1. Preheat your Air Fryer to 160°C (320°F) for 5 minutes.
2. In a large bowl, whisk together flour, sugar, baking powder, and salt.
3. In another bowl, beat egg, then stir in milk, vegetable oil, and vanilla extract.
4. Pour the wet ingredients into the dry ingredients and mix until just combined.
5. Gently fold in the chocolate chips.
6. Line muffin cups with paper liners and fill each about 2/3 full with batter.
7. Place the muffin cups in the Air Fryer basket, ensuring space between each muffin for air circulation.
8. Air fry at 160°C (320°F) for 18-20 minutes or until a toothpick inserted into the center comes out clean.
9. Once done, remove muffins from the Air Fryer and let them cool slightly before serving.

Nutritional Info: Calories: 220 | Fat: 11g | Carbs: 28g | Protein: 3g

Air Fryer Function Used: Bake

Air Fryer Cranberry Orange Muffins

Prep: 15 mins | Cook: 20 mins | Serves: 12 muffins

Ingredients:

- 250g (2 cups) all-purpose flour
- 100g (½ cup) granulated sugar
- 2 tsp baking powder
- ¼ tsp salt
- 1 large egg
- 120ml (½ cup) milk
- 120ml (½ cup) vegetable oil
- 1 tsp vanilla extract
- Zest of 1 orange
- 120g (1 cup) dried cranberries

Instructions:

1. Preheat your Air Fryer to 160°C (320°F) for 5 minutes.
2. In a large bowl, whisk together flour, sugar, baking powder, and salt.
3. In another bowl, beat egg, then stir in milk, vegetable oil, vanilla extract, and orange zest.
4. Pour the wet ingredients into the dry ingredients and mix until just combined.
5. Gently fold in the dried cranberries.
6. Line muffin cups with paper liners and fill each about 2/3 full with batter.
7. Place the muffin cups in the Air Fryer basket, ensuring space between each muffin for air circulation.
8. Air fry at 160°C (320°F) for 18-20 minutes or until a toothpick inserted into the center comes out clean.
9. Once done, remove muffins from the Air Fryer and let them cool slightly before serving.

Nutritional Info: Calories: 210 | Fat: 11g | Carbs: 26g | Protein: 3g

Air Fryer Function Used: Bake

Air Fryer Apple Cinnamon Muffins

Prep: 15 mins | Cook: 20 mins | Serves: 12 muffins

Ingredients:

- 250g (2 cups) all-purpose flour
- 100g (½ cup) granulated sugar
- 2 tsp baking powder
- ¼ tsp salt
- 1 large egg
- 120ml (½ cup) milk
- 120ml (½ cup) vegetable oil
- 1 tsp vanilla extract
- 1 tsp ground cinnamon
- 1 apple, peeled, cored, and diced

Instructions:

1. Preheat your Air Fryer to 160°C (320°F) for 5 minutes.
2. In a large bowl, whisk together flour, sugar, baking powder, salt, and ground cinnamon.
3. In another bowl, beat egg, then stir in milk, vegetable oil, and vanilla extract.
4. Pour the wet ingredients into the dry ingredients and mix until just combined.
5. Gently fold in the diced apple.
6. Line muffin cups with paper liners and fill each about 2/3 full with batter.
7. Place the muffin cups in the Air Fryer basket, ensuring space between each muffin for air circulation.
8. Air fry at 160°C (320°F) for 18-20 minutes or until a toothpick inserted into the center comes out clean.
9. Once done, remove muffins from the Air Fryer and let them cool slightly before serving.

Nutritional Info: Calories: 200 | Fat: 10g | Carbs: 25g | Protein: 3g

Air Fryer Function Used: Bake

Air Fryer Pumpkin Spice Muffins

Prep: 15 mins | Cook: 20 mins | Serves: 12 muffins

Ingredients:
- 250g (2 cups) all-purpose flour
- 100g (½ cup) granulated sugar
- 2 tsp baking powder
- ¼ tsp salt
- 1 tsp ground cinnamon
- ½ tsp ground nutmeg
- ½ tsp ground ginger
- ¼ tsp ground cloves
- 1 large egg
- 120ml (½ cup) milk
- 120ml (½ cup) vegetable oil
- 200g (1 cup) pumpkin puree

Instructions:
1. Preheat your Air Fryer to 160°C (320°F) for 5 minutes.
2. In a large bowl, whisk together flour, sugar, baking powder, salt, and spices.
3. In another bowl, beat egg, then stir in milk, vegetable oil, and pumpkin puree.
4. Pour the wet ingredients into the dry ingredients and mix until just combined.
5. Line muffin cups with paper liners and fill each about 2/3 full with batter.
6. Place the muffin cups in the Air Fryer basket, ensuring space between each muffin for air circulation.
7. Air fry at 160°C (320°F) for 18-20 minutes or until a toothpick inserted into the center comes out clean.
8. Once done, remove muffins from the Air Fryer and let them cool slightly before serving.

Nutritional Info: Calories: 190 | Fat: 9g | Carbs: 25g | Protein: 3g

Air Fryer Function Used: Bake

Air Fryer Zucchini Bread Muffins

Prep: 15 mins | Cook: 20 mins | Serves: 12 muffins

Ingredients:
- 200g (1 ½ cups) all-purpose flour
- 100g (½ cup) granulated sugar
- 1 tsp baking powder
- ½ tsp baking soda
- ¼ tsp salt
- 1 tsp ground cinnamon
- 2 large eggs
- 120ml (½ cup) vegetable oil
- 120ml (½ cup) milk
- 1 tsp vanilla extract
- 200g (1 cup) grated zucchini

Instructions:
1. Preheat your Air Fryer to 160°C (320°F) for 5 minutes.
2. In a large bowl, whisk together flour, sugar, baking powder, baking soda, salt, and cinnamon.
3. In another bowl, beat eggs, then stir in vegetable oil, milk, and vanilla extract.
4. Pour the wet ingredients into the dry ingredients and mix until just combined.
5. Gently fold in the grated zucchini.
6. Line muffin cups with paper liners and fill each about 2/3 full with batter.
7. Place the muffin cups in the Air Fryer basket, ensuring space between each muffin for air circulation.
8. Air fry at 160°C (320°F) for 18-20 minutes or until a toothpick inserted into the center comes out clean.
9. Once done, remove muffins from the Air Fryer and let them cool slightly before serving.

Nutritional Info: Calories: 180 | Fat: 9g | Carbs: 22g | Protein: 3g

Air Fryer Function Used: Bake

Air Fryer Raspberry White Chocolate Muffins

Prep: 15 mins | Cook: 20 mins | Serves: 12 muffins

Ingredients:

- 250g (2 cups) all-purpose flour
- 100g (½ cup) granulated sugar
- 2 tsp baking powder
- ¼ tsp salt
- 1 large egg
- 120ml (½ cup) milk
- 120ml (½ cup) vegetable oil
- 1 tsp vanilla extract
- 150g (1 cup) fresh raspberries
- 100g (¾ cup) white chocolate chips

Instructions:

1. Preheat your Air Fryer to 160°C (320°F) for 5 minutes.
2. In a large bowl, whisk together flour, sugar, baking powder, and salt.
3. In another bowl, beat egg, then stir in milk, vegetable oil, and vanilla extract.
4. Pour the wet ingredients into the dry ingredients and mix until just combined.
5. Gently fold in the raspberries and white chocolate chips.
6. Line muffin cups with paper liners and fill each about 2/3 full with batter.
7. Place the muffin cups in the Air Fryer basket, ensuring space between each muffin for air circulation.
8. Air fry at 160°C (320°F) for 18-20 minutes or until a toothpick inserted into the center comes out clean.
9. Once done, remove muffins from the Air Fryer and let them cool slightly before serving.

Nutritional Info: Calories: 200 | Fat: 10g | Carbs: 26g | Protein: 3g

Air Fryer Function Used: Bake

Air Fryer Cinnamon Crumb Cake Muffins

Prep: 15 mins | Cook: 20 mins | Serves: 12 muffins

Ingredients:

- 250g (2 cups) all-purpose flour
- 150g (¾ cup) granulated sugar
- 1 ½ tsp baking powder
- ½ tsp baking soda
- ¼ tsp salt
- 1 large egg
- 120ml (½ cup) milk
- 120ml (½ cup) vegetable oil
- 1 tsp vanilla extract
- 1 tsp ground cinnamon
- 100g (½ cup) packed brown sugar
- 2 tbsp unsalted butter, melted

Instructions:

1. Preheat your Air Fryer to 160°C (320°F) for 5 minutes.
2. In a large bowl, whisk together flour, granulated sugar, baking powder, baking soda, salt, and ground cinnamon.
3. In another bowl, beat egg, then stir in milk, vegetable oil, and vanilla extract.
4. Pour the wet ingredients into the dry ingredients and mix until just combined.
5. In a small bowl, mix together brown sugar and melted butter to make the crumb topping.
6. Line muffin cups with paper liners and fill each about 2/3 full with batter.
7. Sprinkle the crumb topping evenly over each muffin.
8. Place the muffin cups in the Air Fryer basket, ensuring space between each muffin for air circulation.
9. Air fry at 160°C (320°F) for 18-20 minutes or until a toothpick inserted into the center comes out clean.
10. Once done, remove muffins from the Air Fryer and let them cool slightly before serving.

Nutritional Info: Calories: 220 | Fat: 10g | Carbs: 30g | Protein: 3g

Air Fryer Function Used: Bake

Air Fryer Lemon Poppy Seed Muffins

Prep: 15 mins | Cook: 20 mins | Serves: 12 muffins

Ingredients:

- 250g (2 cups) all-purpose flour
- 150g (¾ cup) granulated sugar
- 1 ½ tsp baking powder
- ½ tsp baking soda
- ¼ tsp salt
- Zest of 1 lemon
- 1 tbsp poppy seeds
- 1 large egg
- 120ml (½ cup) milk
- 120ml (½ cup) vegetable oil
- 1 tsp vanilla extract
- 2 tbsp lemon juice

Instructions:

1. Preheat your Air Fryer to 160°C (320°F) for 5 minutes.
2. In a large bowl, whisk together flour, sugar, baking powder, baking soda, salt, lemon zest, and poppy seeds.
3. In another bowl, beat egg, then stir in milk, vegetable oil, vanilla extract, and lemon juice.
4. Pour the wet ingredients into the dry ingredients and mix until just combined.
5. Line muffin cups with paper liners and fill each about 2/3 full with batter.
6. Place the muffin cups in the Air Fryer basket, ensuring space between each muffin for air circulation.
7. Air fry at 160°C (320°F) for 18-20 minutes or until a toothpick inserted into the center comes out clean.
8. Once done, remove muffins from the Air Fryer and let them cool slightly before serving.

Nutritional Info: Calories: 200 | Fat: 10g | Carbs: 25g | Protein: 3g

Air Fryer Function Used: Bake

Air Fryer Double Chocolate Muffins

Prep: 15 mins | Cook: 20 mins | Serves: 12 muffins

Ingredients:
- 250g (2 cups) all-purpose flour
- 100g (½ cup) granulated sugar
- 50g (½ cup) unsweetened cocoa powder
- 2 tsp baking powder
- ¼ tsp baking soda
- ¼ tsp salt
- 1 large egg
- 120ml (½ cup) milk
- 120ml (½ cup) vegetable oil
- 1 tsp vanilla extract
- 100g (¾ cup) chocolate chips

Instructions:
1. Preheat your Air Fryer to 160°C (320°F) for 5 minutes.
2. In a large bowl, whisk together flour, sugar, cocoa powder, baking powder, baking soda, and salt.
3. In another bowl, beat egg, then stir in milk, vegetable oil, and vanilla extract.
4. Pour the wet ingredients into the dry ingredients and mix until just combined.
5. Gently fold in the chocolate chips.
6. Line muffin cups with paper liners and fill each about 2/3 full with batter.
7. Place the muffin cups in the Air Fryer basket, ensuring space between each muffin for air circulation.
8. Air fry at 160°C (320°F) for 18-20 minutes or until a toothpick inserted into the center comes out clean.
9. Once done, remove muffins from the Air Fryer and let them cool slightly before serving.

Nutritional Info: Calories: 220 | Fat: 11g | Carbs: 29g | Protein: 3g

Air Fryer Function Used: Bake

Air Fryer Bran Muffins

Prep: 15 mins | Cook: 20 mins | Serves: 12 muffins

Ingredients:

- 150g (1 ½ cups) wheat bran
- 240ml (1 cup) milk
- 1 large egg
- 80ml (⅓ cup) vegetable oil
- 80g (⅓ cup) molasses or honey
- 100g (½ cup) brown sugar
- 1 tsp vanilla extract
- 125g (1 cup) all-purpose flour
- 1 tsp baking powder
- ½ tsp baking soda
- ¼ tsp salt

Instructions:

1. Preheat your Air Fryer to 160°C (320°F) for 5 minutes.
2. In a large bowl, mix wheat bran and milk. Let it sit for 10 minutes to soften.
3. In another bowl, beat egg, then stir in vegetable oil, molasses or honey, brown sugar, and vanilla extract.
4. Add the wet ingredients to the softened bran mixture and mix well.
5. In a separate bowl, sift together flour, baking powder, baking soda, and salt.
6. Gradually add the dry ingredients to the wet ingredients, stirring until just combined.
7. Line muffin cups with paper liners and fill each about 2/3 full with batter.
8. Place the muffin cups in the Air Fryer basket, ensuring space between each muffin for air circulation.
9. Air fry at 160°C (320°F) for 18-20 minutes or until a toothpick inserted into the center comes out clean.
10. Once done, remove muffins from the Air Fryer and let them cool slightly before serving.

Nutritional Info: Calories: 180 | Fat: 6g | Carbs: 30g | Protein: 4g

Air Fryer Function Used: Bake

CHAPTER FOUR: BUNDT AND LOAF CAKE BEAUTIES

Air Fryer Classic Bundt Cake

Prep: 15 mins | Cook: 35 mins | Serves: 8-10 slices

Ingredients:
- 200g (1 ¾ cups) all-purpose flour
- 200g (1 cup) granulated sugar
- 3 large eggs
- 120ml (½ cup) vegetable oil
- 120ml (½ cup) milk
- 1 tsp vanilla extract
- 2 tsp baking powder
- ¼ tsp salt

Instructions:
1. Preheat your Air Fryer to 160°C (320°F) for 5 minutes.
2. In a large bowl, whisk together eggs and sugar until pale and fluffy.
3. Gradually add vegetable oil, milk, and vanilla extract, mixing well after each addition.
4. Sift in flour, baking powder, and salt, then fold gently until just combined.
5. Grease and flour a Bundt cake pan.
6. Pour the batter into the prepared pan, spreading it evenly.
7. Place the pan in the Air Fryer basket, ensuring there is space around it for proper air circulation.
8. Air fry at 160°C (320°F) for 35 minutes or until a toothpick inserted into the center comes out clean.
9. Once done, remove the Bundt cake from the Air Fryer and let it cool in the pan for 10 minutes before transferring it to a wire rack to cool completely.

Nutritional Info: Calories: 220 | Fat: 10g | Carbs: 28g | Protein: 4g

Air Fryer Function Used: Bake

Air Fryer Lemon Bundt Cake

Prep: 20 mins | Cook: 40 mins | Serves: 8-10 slices

Ingredients:

- 200g (1 ¾ cups) all-purpose flour
- 200g (1 cup) granulated sugar
- 3 large eggs
- 120ml (½ cup) vegetable oil
- 120ml (½ cup) milk
- Zest of 2 lemons
- Juice of 1 lemon
- 1 tsp vanilla extract
- 2 tsp baking powder
- ¼ tsp salt

Instructions:

1. Preheat your Air Fryer to 160°C (320°F) for 5 minutes.
2. In a large bowl, whisk together eggs and sugar until pale and fluffy.
3. Gradually add vegetable oil, milk, lemon zest, lemon juice, and vanilla extract, mixing well after each addition.
4. Sift in flour, baking powder, and salt, then fold gently until just combined.
5. Grease and flour a Bundt cake pan.
6. Pour the batter into the prepared pan, spreading it evenly.
7. Place the pan in the Air Fryer basket, ensuring there is space around it for proper air circulation.
8. Air fry at 160°C (320°F) for 40 minutes or until a toothpick inserted into the center comes out clean.
9. Once done, remove the Bundt cake from the Air Fryer and let it cool in the pan for 10 minutes before transferring it to a wire rack to cool completely.

Nutritional Info: Calories: 230 | Fat: 11g | Carbs: 30g | Protein: 4g

Air Fryer Function Used: Bake

Air Fryer Chocolate Bundt Cake

Prep: 20 mins | Cook: 40 mins | Serves: 8-10 slices

Ingredients:

- 200g (1 ¾ cups) all-purpose flour
- 200g (1 cup) granulated sugar
- 3 large eggs
- 120ml (½ cup) vegetable oil
- 120ml (½ cup) milk
- 50g (½ cup) cocoa powder
- 1 tsp vanilla extract
- 2 tsp baking powder
- ¼ tsp salt

Instructions:

1. Preheat your Air Fryer to 160°C (320°F) for 5 minutes.
2. In a large bowl, whisk together eggs and sugar until pale and fluffy.
3. Gradually add vegetable oil, milk, cocoa powder, and vanilla extract, mixing well after each addition.
4. Sift in flour, baking powder, and salt, then fold gently until just combined.
5. Grease and flour a Bundt cake pan.
6. Pour the batter into the prepared pan, spreading it evenly.
7. Place the pan in the Air Fryer basket, ensuring there is space around it for proper air circulation.
8. Air fry at 160°C (320°F) for 40 minutes or until a toothpick inserted into the center comes out clean.
9. Once done, remove the Bundt cake from the Air Fryer and let it cool in the pan for 10 minutes before transferring it to a wire rack to cool completely.

Nutritional Info: Calories: 240 | Fat: 12g | Carbs: 31g | Protein: 4g

Air Fryer Function Used: Bake

Air Fryer Pumpkin Bread

Prep: 15 mins | Cook: 50 mins | Serves: 8-10 slices

Ingredients:

- 250g (2 cups) all-purpose flour
- 200g (1 cup) granulated sugar
- 1 tsp baking soda
- ½ tsp baking powder
- ½ tsp salt
- 1 tsp ground cinnamon
- ½ tsp ground nutmeg
- ½ tsp ground cloves
- 2 large eggs
- 200g (1 cup) canned pumpkin puree
- 120ml (½ cup) vegetable oil
- 60ml (¼ cup) milk
- 1 tsp vanilla extract

Instructions:

1. Preheat your Air Fryer to 160°C (320°F) for 5 minutes.
2. In a large bowl, whisk together flour, sugar, baking soda, baking powder, salt, cinnamon, nutmeg, and cloves.
3. In another bowl, beat eggs, then stir in pumpkin puree, vegetable oil, milk, and vanilla extract.
4. Pour the wet ingredients into the dry ingredients and mix until just combined.
5. Grease and flour a loaf pan.
6. Pour the batter into the prepared loaf pan, spreading it evenly.
7. Place the loaf pan in the Air Fryer basket, ensuring there is space around it for proper air circulation.
8. Air fry at 160°C (320°F) for 50 minutes or until a toothpick inserted into the center comes out clean.
9. Once done, remove the pumpkin bread from the Air Fryer and let it cool in the pan for 10 minutes before transferring it to a wire rack to cool completely.

Nutritional Info: Calories: 220 | Fat: 10g | Carbs: 30g | Protein: 3g

Air Fryer Function Used: Bake

Air Fryer Banana Bread

Prep: 15 mins | Cook: 50 mins | Serves: 8-10 slices

Ingredients:
- 3 ripe bananas, mashed
- 200g (1 cup) granulated sugar
- 2 large eggs
- 120ml (½ cup) vegetable oil
- 60ml (¼ cup) milk
- 1 tsp vanilla extract
- 250g (2 cups) all-purpose flour
- 1 tsp baking soda
- ½ tsp salt

Instructions:
1. Preheat your Air Fryer to 160°C (320°F) for 5 minutes.
2. In a large bowl, mix mashed bananas and sugar until well combined.
3. Add eggs, vegetable oil, milk, and vanilla extract, and mix until smooth.
4. Sift in flour, baking soda, and salt, then fold gently until just combined.
5. Grease and flour a loaf pan.
6. Pour the batter into the prepared loaf pan, spreading it evenly.
7. Place the loaf pan in the Air Fryer basket, ensuring there is space around it for proper air circulation.
8. Air fry at 160°C (320°F) for 50 minutes or until a toothpick inserted into the center comes out clean.
9. Once done, remove the banana bread from the Air Fryer and let it cool in the pan for 10 minutes before transferring it to a wire rack to cool completely.

Nutritional Info: Calories: 210 | Fat: 9g | Carbs: 30g | Protein: 3g

Air Fryer Function Used: Bake

Air Fryer Zucchini Bread

Prep: 15 mins | Cook: 50 mins | Serves: 8-10 slices

Ingredients:

- 200g (1 ¾ cups) all-purpose flour
- 150g (¾ cup) granulated sugar
- 1 tsp baking powder
- ½ tsp baking soda
- ½ tsp salt
- 1 tsp ground cinnamon
- 2 large eggs
- 120ml (½ cup) vegetable oil
- 60ml (¼ cup) milk
- 1 tsp vanilla extract
- 200g (1 ½ cups) grated zucchini
- 50g (½ cup) chopped nuts (optional)

Instructions:

1. Preheat your Air Fryer to 160°C (320°F) for 5 minutes.
2. In a large bowl, whisk together eggs, sugar, vegetable oil, milk, and vanilla extract until well combined.
3. Stir in grated zucchini.
4. In a separate bowl, sift together flour, baking powder, baking soda, salt, and cinnamon.
5. Gradually add the dry ingredients to the wet ingredients, mixing until just combined.
6. If using, fold in chopped nuts.
7. Grease and flour a loaf pan.
8. Pour the batter into the prepared loaf pan, spreading it evenly.
9. Place the loaf pan in the Air Fryer basket, ensuring there is space around it for proper air circulation.
10. Air fry at 160°C (320°F) for 50 minutes or until a toothpick inserted into the center comes out clean.
11. Once done, remove the zucchini bread from the Air Fryer and let it cool in the pan for 10 minutes before transferring it to a wire rack to cool completely.

Nutritional Info: Calories: 200 | Fat: 10g | Carbs: 25g | Protein: 3g

Air Fryer Function Used: Bake

Air Fryer Cranberry Orange Bread

Prep: 15 mins | Cook: 50 mins | Serves: 8-10 slices

Ingredients:

- 250g (2 cups) all-purpose flour
- 150g (¾ cup) granulated sugar
- 1 tsp baking powder
- ½ tsp baking soda
- ½ tsp salt
- Zest of 1 orange
- 120ml (½ cup) freshly squeezed orange juice
- 2 large eggs
- 120ml (½ cup) vegetable oil
- 50g (½ cup) dried cranberries

Instructions:

1. Preheat your Air Fryer to 160°C (320°F) for 5 minutes.
2. In a large bowl, whisk together flour, sugar, baking powder, baking soda, salt, and orange zest.
3. In another bowl, beat eggs, then stir in orange juice and vegetable oil.
4. Pour the wet ingredients into the dry ingredients and mix until just combined.
5. Gently fold in dried cranberries.
6. Grease and flour a loaf pan.
7. Pour the batter into the prepared loaf pan, spreading it evenly.
8. Place the loaf pan in the Air Fryer basket, ensuring there is space around it for proper air circulation.
9. Air fry at 160°C (320°F) for 50 minutes or until a toothpick inserted into the center comes out clean.
10. Once done, remove the cranberry orange bread from the Air Fryer and let it cool in the pan for 10 minutes before transferring it to a wire rack to cool completely.

Nutritional Info: Calories: 210 | Fat: 9g | Carbs: 28g | Protein: 3g

Air Fryer Function Used: Bake

Air Fryer Apple Cinnamon Bread

Prep: 15 mins | Cook: 50 mins | Serves: 8-10 slices

Ingredients:

- 250g (2 cups) all-purpose flour
- 150g (¾ cup) granulated sugar
- 1 tsp baking powder
- ½ tsp baking soda
- ½ tsp salt
- 1 tsp ground cinnamon
- 2 large eggs
- 120ml (½ cup) vegetable oil
- 60ml (¼ cup) milk
- 1 tsp vanilla extract
- 2 apples, peeled, cored, and diced

Instructions:

1. Preheat your Air Fryer to 160°C (320°F) for 5 minutes.
2. In a large bowl, whisk together eggs, sugar, vegetable oil, milk, and vanilla extract until well combined.
3. In another bowl, combine flour, baking powder, baking soda, salt, and ground cinnamon.
4. Gradually add the dry ingredients to the wet ingredients, mixing until just combined.
5. Gently fold in the diced apples.
6. Grease and flour a loaf pan.
7. Pour the batter into the prepared loaf pan, spreading it evenly.
8. Place the loaf pan in the Air Fryer basket, ensuring there is space around it for proper air circulation.
9. Air fry at 160°C (320°F) for 50 minutes or until a toothpick inserted into the center comes out clean.
10. Once done, remove the apple cinnamon bread from the Air Fryer and let it cool in the pan for 10 minutes before transferring it to a wire rack to cool completely.

Nutritional Info: Calories: 220 | Fat: 10g | Carbs: 30g | Protein: 3g

Air Fryer Function Used: Bake

Air Fryer Gingerbread Loaf

Prep: 15 mins | Cook: 50 mins | Serves: 8-10 slices

Ingredients:
- 250g (2 cups) all-purpose flour
- 100g (½ cup) granulated sugar
- 1 tsp baking soda
- 1 ½ tsp ground ginger
- 1 tsp ground cinnamon
- ½ tsp ground cloves
- ½ tsp salt
- 2 large eggs
- 120ml (½ cup) molasses
- 120ml (½ cup) vegetable oil
- 120ml (½ cup) hot water

Instructions:
1. Preheat your Air Fryer to 160°C (320°F) for 5 minutes.
2. In a large bowl, whisk together flour, sugar, baking soda, ginger, cinnamon, cloves, and salt.
3. In another bowl, beat eggs, then stir in molasses and vegetable oil.
4. Gradually add the wet ingredients to the dry ingredients, mixing until just combined.
5. Gradually add hot water to the batter, mixing until smooth.
6. Grease and flour a loaf pan.
7. Pour the batter into the prepared loaf pan, spreading it evenly.
8. Place the loaf pan in the Air Fryer basket, ensuring there is space around it for proper air circulation.
9. Air fry at 160°C (320°F) for 50 minutes or until a toothpick inserted into the center comes out clean.
10. Once done, remove the gingerbread loaf from the Air Fryer and let it cool in the pan for 10 minutes before transferring it to a wire rack to cool completely.

Nutritional Info: Calories: 220 | Fat: 10g | Carbs: 30g | Protein: 3g

Air Fryer Function Used: Bake

Air Fryer Streusel Coffee Cake

Prep: 20 mins | Cook: 40 mins | Serves: 8-10 slices

Ingredients:
- 250g (2 cups) all-purpose flour
- 150g (¾ cup) granulated sugar
- 1 tsp baking powder
- ½ tsp baking soda
- ½ tsp salt
- 120ml (½ cup) vegetable oil
- 120ml (½ cup) sour cream
- 2 large eggs
- 1 tsp vanilla extract

For Streusel Topping:

- 50g (¼ cup) granulated sugar
- 50g (¼ cup) packed brown sugar
- 1 tsp ground cinnamon
- 50g (⅓ cup) all-purpose flour
- 60g (¼ cup) unsalted butter, melted

Instructions:
1. Preheat your Air Fryer to 160°C (320°F) for 5 minutes.
2. In a large bowl, whisk together flour, sugar, baking powder, baking soda, and salt.
3. In another bowl, mix together vegetable oil, sour cream, eggs, and vanilla extract until well combined.
4. Gradually add the wet ingredients to the dry ingredients, mixing until just combined.
5. In a separate bowl, combine all streusel topping ingredients until crumbly.
6. Grease and flour a loaf pan.
7. Pour half of the batter into the prepared loaf pan, spreading it evenly.
8. Sprinkle half of the streusel topping over the batter.
9. Pour the remaining batter over the streusel layer, spreading it evenly.
10. Sprinkle the remaining streusel topping over the top.
11. Place the loaf pan in the Air Fryer basket, ensuring there is space around it for proper air circulation.
12. Air fry at 160°C (320°F) for 40 minutes or until a toothpick inserted into the center comes out clean.

13. Once done, remove the streusel coffee cake from the Air Fryer and let it cool in the pan for 10 minutes before transferring it to a wire rack to cool completely.

Nutritional Info: Calories: 280 | Fat: 14g | Carbs: 36g | Protein: 4g

Air Fryer Function Used: Bake

Air Fryer Walnut Bread

Prep: 15 mins | Cook: 50 mins | Serves: 8-10 slices

Ingredients:
- 250g (2 cups) all-purpose flour
- 150g (¾ cup) granulated sugar
- 1 tsp baking powder
- ½ tsp baking soda
- ½ tsp salt
- 120ml (½ cup) vegetable oil
- 120ml (½ cup) milk
- 2 large eggs
- 1 tsp vanilla extract
- 100g (1 cup) chopped walnuts

1. *Instructions:*
1. Preheat your Air Fryer to 160°C (320°F) for 5 minutes.
2. In a large bowl, whisk together flour, sugar, baking powder, baking soda, and salt.
3. In another bowl, mix together vegetable oil, milk, eggs, and vanilla extract until well combined.
4. Gradually add the wet ingredients to the dry ingredients, mixing until just combined.
5. Gently fold in the chopped walnuts.
6. Grease and flour a loaf pan.
7. Pour the batter into the prepared loaf pan, spreading it evenly.
8. Place the loaf pan in the Air Fryer basket, ensuring there is space around it for proper air circulation.
9. Air fry at 160°C (320°F) for 50 minutes or until a toothpick inserted into the center comes out clean.

10. Once done, remove the walnut bread from the Air Fryer and let it cool in the pan for 10 minutes before transferring it to a wire rack to cool completely.

Nutritional Info: Calories: 250 | Fat: 12g | Carbs: 32g | Protein: 4g

Air Fryer Function Used: Bake

Air Fryer Coconut Bread

Prep: 15 mins | Cook: 50 mins | Serves: 8-10 slices

Ingredients:
- 250g (2 cups) all-purpose flour
- 150g (¾ cup) granulated sugar
- 1 tsp baking powder
- ½ tsp baking soda
- ½ tsp salt
- 120ml (½ cup) coconut milk
- 120ml (½ cup) vegetable oil
- 2 large eggs
- 1 tsp vanilla extract
- 50g (½ cup) shredded coconut

Instructions:
1. Preheat your Air Fryer to 160°C (320°F) for 5 minutes.
2. In a large bowl, whisk together flour, sugar, baking powder, baking soda, and salt.
3. In another bowl, mix together coconut milk, vegetable oil, eggs, and vanilla extract until well combined.
4. Gradually add the wet ingredients to the dry ingredients, mixing until just combined.
5. Gently fold in the shredded coconut.
6. Grease and flour a loaf pan.
7. Pour the batter into the prepared loaf pan, spreading it evenly.
8. Place the loaf pan in the Air Fryer basket, ensuring there is space around it for proper air circulation.
9. Air fry at 160°C (320°F) for 50 minutes or until a toothpick inserted into the center comes out clean.

10. Once done, remove the coconut bread from the Air Fryer and let it cool in the pan for 10 minutes before transferring it to a wire rack to cool completely.

Nutritional Info: Calories: 240 | Fat: 11g | Carbs: 31g | Protein: 3g

Air Fryer Function Used: Bake

Air Fryer Marble Bundt Cake

Prep: 20 mins | Cook: 40 mins | Serves: 8-10 slices

Ingredients:
- 250g (2 cups) all-purpose flour
- 150g (¾ cup) granulated sugar
- 3 large eggs
- 120ml (½ cup) vegetable oil
- 120ml (½ cup) milk
- 2 tsp baking powder
- ¼ tsp salt
- 2 tbsp unsweetened cocoa powder

Instructions:
1. Preheat your Air Fryer to 160°C (320°F) for 5 minutes.
2. In a large bowl, whisk together eggs and sugar until pale and fluffy.
3. Gradually add vegetable oil and milk, mixing well after each addition.
4. Sift in flour, baking powder, and salt, then fold gently until just combined.
5. Divide the batter into two equal portions.
6. Mix cocoa powder with one portion of the batter until well combined.
7. Grease and flour a Bundt cake pan.
8. Alternately spoon dollops of the plain and chocolate batter into the prepared pan.
9. Use a skewer or knife to swirl the batters together gently to create a marbled effect.
10. Place the pan in the Air Fryer basket, ensuring there is space around it for proper air circulation.
11. Air fry at 160°C (320°F) for 40 minutes or until a toothpick inserted into the center comes out clean.

12. Once done, remove the marble Bundt cake from the Air Fryer and let it cool in the pan for 10 minutes before transferring it to a wire rack to cool completely.

Nutritional Info: Calories: 230 | Fat: 10g | Carbs: 31g | Protein: 4g

Air Fryer Function Used: Bake

Air Fryer Pecan Pie Bundt Cake

Prep: 20 mins | Cook: 40 mins | Serves: 8-10 slices

Ingredients:
- 250g (2 cups) all-purpose flour
- 150g (¾ cup) granulated sugar
- 3 large eggs
- 120ml (½ cup) vegetable oil
- 120ml (½ cup) milk
- 2 tsp baking powder
- ¼ tsp salt
- 100g (1 cup) chopped pecans

Instructions:
1. Preheat your Air Fryer to 160°C (320°F) for 5 minutes.
2. In a large bowl, whisk together eggs and sugar until pale and fluffy.
3. Gradually add vegetable oil and milk, mixing well after each addition.
4. Sift in flour, baking powder, and salt, then fold gently until just combined.
5. Gently fold in chopped pecans.
6. Grease and flour a Bundt cake pan.
7. Pour the batter into the prepared pan, spreading it evenly.
8. Place the pan in the Air Fryer basket, ensuring there is space around it for proper air circulation.
9. Air fry at 160°C (320°F) for 40 minutes or until a toothpick inserted into the center comes out clean.
10. Once done, remove the pecan pie Bundt cake from the Air Fryer and let it cool in the pan for 10 minutes before transferring it to a wire rack to cool completely.

Nutritional Info: Calories: 240 | Fat: 11g | Carbs: 31g | Protein: 4g

Air Fryer Function Used: Bake

Air Fryer Raspberry Swirl Bread

Prep: 15 mins | Cook: 50 mins | Serves: 8-10 slices

Ingredients:

- 250g (2 cups) all-purpose flour
- 150g (¾ cup) granulated sugar
- 3 large eggs
- 120ml (½ cup) vegetable oil
- 120ml (½ cup) milk
- 2 tsp baking powder
- ¼ tsp salt
- 100g (1 cup) fresh or frozen raspberries

Instructions:

1. Preheat your Air Fryer to 160°C (320°F) for 5 minutes.
2. In a large bowl, whisk together eggs and sugar until pale and fluffy.
3. Gradually add vegetable oil and milk, mixing well after each addition.
4. Sift in flour, baking powder, and salt, then fold gently until just combined.
5. Grease and flour a loaf pan.
6. Pour the batter into the prepared loaf pan, spreading it evenly.
7. Scatter raspberries evenly over the batter.
8. Use a knife to gently swirl the raspberries into the batter.
9. Place the loaf pan in the Air Fryer basket, ensuring there is space around it for proper air circulation.
10. Air fry at 160°C (320°F) for 50 minutes or until a toothpick inserted into the center comes out clean.
11. Once done, remove the raspberry swirl bread from the Air Fryer and let it cool in the pan for 10 minutes before transferring it to a wire rack to cool completely.

Nutritional Info: Calories: 230 | Fat: 10g | Carbs: 31g | Protein: 4g

Air Fryer Function Used: Bake

Air Fryer Lemon Blueberry Loaf

Prep: 15 mins | Cook: 50 mins | Serves: 8-10 slices

Ingredients:

- 250g (2 cups) all-purpose flour
- 150g (¾ cup) granulated sugar
- 3 large eggs
- 120ml (½ cup) vegetable oil
- 120ml (½ cup) milk
- Zest of 1 lemon
- Juice of 1 lemon
- 2 tsp baking powder
- ¼ tsp salt
- 150g (1 cup) fresh or frozen blueberries

Instructions:

1. Preheat your Air Fryer to 160°C (320°F) for 5 minutes.
2. In a large bowl, whisk together eggs and sugar until pale and fluffy.
3. Gradually add vegetable oil, milk, lemon zest, and lemon juice, mixing well after each addition.
4. Sift in flour, baking powder, and salt, then fold gently until just combined.
5. Gently fold in the blueberries.
6. Grease and flour a loaf pan.
7. Pour the batter into the prepared loaf pan, spreading it evenly.
8. Place the loaf pan in the Air Fryer basket, ensuring there is space around it for proper air circulation.
9. Air fry at 160°C (320°F) for 50 minutes or until a toothpick inserted into the center comes out clean.
10. Once done, remove the lemon blueberry loaf from the Air Fryer and let it cool in the pan for 10 minutes before transferring it to a wire rack to cool completely.

Nutritional Info: Calories: 240 | Fat: 11g | Carbs: 31g | Protein: 4g

Air Fryer Function Used: Bake

CHAPTER FIVE: MINI AND BITE-SIZED TREATS

Air Fryer Mini Bundt Cakes

Prep: 15 mins | Cook: 25 mins | Serves: 12 mini bundt cakes

Ingredients:
- 150g (1 ¼ cups) all-purpose flour
- 100g (½ cup) granulated sugar
- 1 tsp baking powder
- ½ tsp baking soda
- Pinch of salt
- 2 large eggs
- 120ml (½ cup) milk
- 60ml (¼ cup) vegetable oil
- 1 tsp vanilla extract

Instructions:
1. Preheat your Air Fryer to 160°C (320°F) for 5 minutes.
2. In a large bowl, whisk together flour, sugar, baking powder, baking soda, and salt.
3. In another bowl, beat eggs, then mix in milk, vegetable oil, and vanilla extract.
4. Pour the wet ingredients into the dry ingredients and stir until just combined.
5. Grease the mini bundt cake molds.
6. Fill each mold with the batter until ¾ full.
7. Place the molds in the Air Fryer basket, ensuring they are not touching.
8. Air fry at 160°C (320°F) for 25 minutes or until a toothpick inserted into the center of a cake comes out clean.
9. Once done, remove the mini bundt cakes from the Air Fryer and let them cool in the molds for 5 minutes.
10. Carefully remove the cakes from the molds and transfer them to a wire rack to cool completely.

Nutritional Info: Calories: 120 | Fat: 4g | Carbs: 18g | Protein: 2g

Air Fryer Function Used: Bake

Air Fryer Cake Pops

Prep: 30 mins | Cook: 20 mins | Serves: 12 cake pops

Ingredients:

- 1 box (250g) cake mix (any flavor)
- Ingredients required by the cake mix (e.g., eggs, oil, water)
- 150g (1 cup) chocolate chips
- Sprinkles or toppings of your choice

Instructions:

1. Prepare the cake mix according to package instructions.
2. Grease and flour a cake pop mold.
3. Fill each cavity with the cake batter.
4. Place the mold in the Air Fryer basket, ensuring it is not touching the sides.
5. Air fry at 160°C (320°F) for 20 minutes or until the cake pops are firm.
6. Once done, remove the cake pops from the Air Fryer and let them cool for 10 minutes.
7. Melt the chocolate chips in the microwave or using a double boiler.
8. Dip the tip of each cake pop stick into the melted chocolate and insert it into the cake pops.
9. Dip each cake pop into the melted chocolate, allowing the excess to drip off.
10. Decorate with sprinkles or toppings of your choice.
11. Place the cake pops on a tray lined with parchment paper and let the chocolate set.

Nutritional Info: Calories: 180 | Fat: 8g | Carbs: 25g | Protein: 2g

Air Fryer Function Used: Bake

Air Fryer Cake Truffles

Prep: 20 mins | Cook: 25 mins | Chilling: 1 hour | Serves: 24 truffles

Ingredients:
- 250g (2 cups) cake crumbs (from any leftover cake or store-bought)
- 120g (½ cup) cream cheese, softened
- 200g (1 ½ cups) chocolate chips
- 1 tbsp vegetable oil
- Sprinkles or cocoa powder for decoration (optional)

Instructions:
1. In a mixing bowl, combine the cake crumbs and softened cream cheese until well blended.
2. Roll the mixture into small balls, about 1 inch in diameter, and place them on a baking sheet lined with parchment paper.
3. Freeze the cake balls for 30 minutes to firm them up.
4. Preheat your Air Fryer to 160°C (320°F) for 5 minutes.
5. In a microwave-safe bowl, melt the chocolate chips with vegetable oil in 30-second intervals, stirring between each interval, until smooth.
6. Using a fork or toothpicks, dip each chilled cake ball into the melted chocolate, ensuring it is evenly coated.
7. Place the coated cake truffles back onto the parchment-lined baking sheet.
8. Optionally, decorate with sprinkles or dust with cocoa powder.
9. Transfer the baking sheet to the Air Fryer basket, ensuring the truffles are not touching.
10. Air fry at 160°C (320°F) for 5 minutes or until the chocolate coating is set.
11. Once done, remove the cake truffles from the Air Fryer and let them cool completely.
12. For best results, refrigerate the cake truffles for at least 1 hour before serving.

Nutritional Info: Calories: 120 | Fat: 8g | Carbs: 12g | Protein: 1g

Air Fryer Function Used: Bake

Air Fryer Mini Cupcakes

Prep: 15 mins | Cook: 15 mins | Serves: 24 mini cupcakes

Ingredients:

- 150g (1 ¼ cups) all-purpose flour
- 100g (½ cup) granulated sugar
- 1 tsp baking powder
- ½ tsp baking soda
- Pinch of salt
- 1 large egg
- 80ml (⅓ cup) vegetable oil
- 80ml (⅓ cup) milk
- 1 tsp vanilla extract

Instructions:

1. Preheat your Air Fryer to 160°C (320°F) for 5 minutes.
2. In a large bowl, whisk together flour, sugar, baking powder, baking soda, and salt.
3. In another bowl, beat the egg, then mix in vegetable oil, milk, and vanilla extract.
4. Pour the wet ingredients into the dry ingredients and stir until just combined.
5. Line a mini cupcake tin with paper liners.
6. Fill each liner with the batter until ¾ full.
7. Place the cupcake tin in the Air Fryer basket, ensuring there is space around each cupcake.
8. Air fry at 160°C (320°F) for 15 minutes or until a toothpick inserted into the center of a cupcake comes out clean.
9. Once done, remove the mini cupcakes from the Air Fryer and let them cool in the tin for 5 minutes.
10. Transfer the cupcakes to a wire rack to cool completely before frosting, if desired.

Nutritional Info: Calories: 80 | Fat: 4g | Carbs: 10g | Protein: 1g

Air Fryer Function Used: Bake

Air Fryer Brownie Bites

Prep: 15 mins | Cook: 15 mins | Serves: 24 brownie bites

Ingredients:

- 100g (½ cup) unsalted butter
- 100g (1 cup) granulated sugar
- 2 large eggs
- 1 tsp vanilla extract
- 40g (⅓ cup) all-purpose flour
- 30g (⅓ cup) unsweetened cocoa powder
- Pinch of salt
- 60g (½ cup) chocolate chips

Instructions:

1. Preheat your Air Fryer to 160°C (320°F) for 5 minutes.
2. In a microwave-safe bowl, melt the butter in the microwave.
3. Stir in sugar until well combined.
4. Beat in eggs, one at a time, followed by vanilla extract.
5. Sift in flour, cocoa powder, and salt. Mix until just combined.
6. Fold in chocolate chips.
7. Grease and flour a mini muffin tin or use paper liners.
8. Spoon the brownie batter into each muffin cup, filling each about ¾ full.
9. Place the muffin tin in the Air Fryer basket, ensuring there is space around each cup.
10. Air fry at 160°C (320°F) for 15 minutes or until the brownies are set.
11. Once done, remove the brownie bites from the Air Fryer and let them cool in the tin for 5 minutes.
12. Transfer the brownie bites to a wire rack to cool completely before serving.

Nutritional Info: Calories: 90 | Fat: 5g | Carbs: 10g | Protein: 1g

Air Fryer Function Used: Bake

Air Fryer Lemon Bars

Prep: 20 mins | Cook: 25 mins | Chill: 2 hours | Serves: 12 bars

Ingredients:
- 150g (1 ¼ cups) all-purpose flour
- 50g (¼ cup) powdered sugar
- 115g (½ cup) unsalted butter, softened
- 200g (1 cup) granulated sugar
- 3 large eggs
- Zest of 2 lemons
- 80ml (⅓ cup) lemon juice
- 2 tbsp all-purpose flour
- Powdered sugar for dusting

Instructions:
1. Preheat your Air Fryer to 160°C (320°F) for 5 minutes.
2. In a mixing bowl, combine flour, powdered sugar, and softened butter until crumbly.
3. Press the mixture into the bottom of a greased and floured square baking pan.
4. Bake the crust in the Air Fryer for 10 minutes.
5. In another bowl, whisk together granulated sugar, eggs, lemon zest, lemon juice, and flour until well combined.
6. Pour the lemon mixture over the partially baked crust.
7. Return the baking pan to the Air Fryer and bake for an additional 15 minutes or until the filling is set.
8. Once done, remove the lemon bars from the Air Fryer and let them cool completely.
9. Chill the lemon bars in the refrigerator for at least 2 hours before slicing.
10. Dust the chilled bars with powdered sugar before serving.

Nutritional Info: Calories: 180 | Fat: 7g | Carbs: 27g | Protein: 2g

Air Fryer Function Used: Bake

Air Fryer Coconut Macaroons

Prep: 15 mins | Cook: 12 mins | Serves: 12 macaroons

Ingredients:
- 200g (2 cups) shredded coconut
- 100g (⅔ cup) granulated sugar
- 2 large egg whites
- 1 tsp vanilla extract
- Pinch of salt
- 100g (½ cup) chocolate chips (optional, for dipping)

Instructions:
1. Preheat your Air Fryer to 160°C (320°F) for 5 minutes.
2. In a mixing bowl, combine shredded coconut, granulated sugar, egg whites, vanilla extract, and salt. Mix until well combined.
3. Using a cookie scoop or spoon, form the coconut mixture into small mounds and place them on a parchment-lined baking sheet.
4. Place the baking sheet in the Air Fryer basket, ensuring there is space around each macaroon.
5. Air fry at 160°C (320°F) for 12 minutes or until the macaroons are golden brown.
6. If desired, melt chocolate chips in the microwave or using a double boiler.
7. Dip the bottom of each cooled macaroon into the melted chocolate, then place them back on the parchment paper to set.
8. Allow the chocolate to set completely before serving.

Nutritional Info: Calories: 120 | Fat: 7g | Carbs: 14g | Protein: 1g

Air Fryer Function Used: Bake

Air Fryer Meringue Kisses

Prep: 15 mins | Cook: 90 mins | Serves: 24 meringue kisses

Ingredients:

- 2 large egg whites
- 100g (½ cup) granulated sugar
- ½ tsp vanilla extract
- Pinch of salt
- Food coloring (optional)

Instructions:

1. Preheat your Air Fryer to 90°C (194°F) for 5 minutes.
2. In a clean, dry mixing bowl, beat the egg whites with an electric mixer until soft peaks form.
3. Gradually add the granulated sugar, vanilla extract, and salt while continuing to beat until stiff peaks form and the mixture is glossy.
4. If using food coloring, gently fold it into the meringue mixture until evenly colored.
5. Transfer the meringue mixture to a piping bag fitted with a star tip.
6. Pipe small kisses onto a parchment-lined baking sheet.
7. Place the baking sheet in the Air Fryer basket, ensuring there is space around each meringue kiss.
8. Air fry at 90°C (194°F) for 90 minutes or until the meringues are dry and crisp.
9. Once done, turn off the Air Fryer and let the meringue kisses cool completely inside the Air Fryer with the door slightly ajar.
10. Once cooled, carefully remove the meringue kisses from the Air Fryer and store them in an airtight container.

Nutritional Info: Calories: 20 | Fat: 0g | Carbs: 5g | Protein: 0g

Air Fryer Function Used: Bake

Air Fryer Madeleines

Prep: 20 mins | Cook: 10 mins | Serves: 12 madeleines

Ingredients:
- 2 large eggs
- 100g (½ cup) granulated sugar
- 120g (1 cup) all-purpose flour
- ½ tsp baking powder
- Pinch of salt
- 115g (½ cup) unsalted butter, melted and cooled
- 1 tsp vanilla extract
- Zest of 1 lemon (optional)

Instructions:
1. Preheat your Air Fryer to 180°C (356°F) for 5 minutes.
2. In a mixing bowl, beat the eggs and sugar together until pale and fluffy.
3. Sift in the flour, baking powder, and salt. Fold gently until just combined.
4. Gradually pour in the melted butter, vanilla extract, and lemon zest (if using). Mix until smooth.
5. Cover the batter and refrigerate for at least 1 hour.
6. Grease the madeleine molds with butter or non-stick spray.
7. Spoon the chilled batter into the molds, filling each about ¾ full.
8. Place the molds in the Air Fryer basket, ensuring there is space between each madeleine.
9. Air fry at 180°C (356°F) for 10 minutes or until the madeleines are golden brown and spring back when lightly touched.
10. Once done, remove the madeleines from the Air Fryer and let them cool in the molds for a few minutes.
11. Gently tap the molds to release the madeleines, then transfer them to a wire rack to cool completely.

Nutritional Info: Calories: 120 | Fat: 6g | Carbs: 15g | Protein: 2g

Air Fryer Function Used: Bake

Air Fryer Financiers

Prep: 15 mins | Cook: 12 mins | Serves: 12 financiers

Ingredients:

- 100g (¾ cup) almond flour
- 50g (½ cup) powdered sugar
- 40g (⅓ cup) all-purpose flour
- 100g (½ cup) unsalted butter, melted and cooled
- 3 large egg whites
- ½ tsp almond extract
- Sliced almonds for garnish (optional)

Instructions:

1. Preheat your Air Fryer to 180°C (356°F) for 5 minutes.
2. In a mixing bowl, combine almond flour, powdered sugar, and all-purpose flour.
3. In another bowl, whisk the egg whites until frothy.
4. Gradually fold the egg whites into the dry ingredients until just combined.
5. Stir in the melted butter and almond extract until smooth.
6. Grease the financier molds with butter or non-stick spray.
7. Spoon the batter into the molds, filling each about ¾ full.
8. Sprinkle sliced almonds on top of each financier if desired.
9. Place the molds in the Air Fryer basket, ensuring there is space between each financier.
10. Air fry at 180°C (356°F) for 12 minutes or until the financiers are golden brown and spring back when lightly touched.
11. Once done, remove the financiers from the Air Fryer and let them cool in the molds for a few minutes.
12. Gently tap the molds to release the financiers, then transfer them to a wire rack to cool completely.

Nutritional Info: Calories: 130 | Fat: 9g | Carbs: 10g | Protein: 3g

Air Fryer Function Used: Bake

Air Fryer Petit Fours

Prep: 30 mins | Cook: 15 mins | Chill: 1 hour | Serves: 24 petit fours

Ingredients:
- 1 sheet of pre-made sponge cake or pound cake
- 120g (1 cup) powdered sugar
- 2-3 tbsp milk
- Food coloring (optional)
- Assorted sprinkles or decorations

Instructions:
1. Preheat your Air Fryer to 160°C (320°F) for 5 minutes.
2. Using a sharp knife, trim the edges of the sponge cake to create straight sides.
3. Cut the cake into small squares or rectangles, about 1 inch in size.
4. In a small bowl, whisk together powdered sugar and milk until smooth. Add food coloring if desired.
5. Dip each cake square into the glaze, allowing any excess to drip off.
6. Place the glazed cake squares on a wire rack set over a baking sheet to catch any drips.
7. Decorate the petit fours with assorted sprinkles or decorations.
8. Transfer the wire rack with the decorated petit fours to the Air Fryer basket.
9. Air fry at 160°C (320°F) for 15 minutes or until the glaze is set.
10. Once done, remove the petit fours from the Air Fryer and let them cool completely.
11. Chill the petit fours in the refrigerator for at least 1 hour before serving to allow the glaze to fully set.

Nutritional Info: Calories: 60 | Fat: 1g | Carbs: 12g | Protein: 1g

Air Fryer Function Used: Bake

Air Fryer Fruit Tarts

Prep: 30 mins | Cook: 15 mins | Chill: 1 hour | Serves: 12 tarts

Ingredients:
- 1 sheet of pre-made puff pastry, thawed
- 200g (1 cup) cream cheese, softened
- 2 tbsp powdered sugar
- Assorted fresh fruits (e.g., strawberries, blueberries, kiwi)
- Apricot jam or honey for glazing

Instructions:
1. Preheat your Air Fryer to 180°C (356°F) for 5 minutes.
2. Roll out the puff pastry sheet on a lightly floured surface.
3. Cut the pastry into circles using a cookie cutter or glass, slightly larger than the wells of your tart molds.
4. Press the pastry circles into greased mini tart molds, trimming any excess pastry.
5. Prick the bottoms of the pastry with a fork to prevent air bubbles.
6. In a mixing bowl, beat together cream cheese and powdered sugar until smooth.
7. Spread a thin layer of the cream cheese mixture onto the bottom of each tart shell.
8. Arrange assorted fresh fruits on top of the cream cheese mixture.
9. Place the tart molds in the Air Fryer basket, ensuring there is space between each tart.
10. Air fry at 180°C (356°F) for 15 minutes or until the pastry is golden brown and crispy.
11. Once done, remove the fruit tarts from the Air Fryer and let them cool in the molds for a few minutes.
12. Gently remove the tarts from the molds and transfer them to a wire rack to cool completely.
13. Heat apricot jam or honey in the microwave for a few seconds until thin. Brush over the tops of the cooled fruit tarts for a glossy finish.
14. Chill the fruit tarts in the refrigerator for at least 1 hour before serving.

Nutritional Info: Calories: 140 | Fat: 8g | Carbs: 15g | Protein: 2g

Air Fryer Function Used: Bake

Air Fryer Cheesecake Bites

Prep: 20 mins | Cook: 25 mins | Chill: 2 hours | Serves: 12 cheesecake bites

Ingredients:
- 200g (1 ½ cups) cream cheese, softened
- 50g (¼ cup) granulated sugar
- 1 large egg
- ½ tsp vanilla extract
- 120ml (½ cup) sour cream
- 1 tbsp all-purpose flour
- Graham cracker crumbs for garnish

Instructions:
1. Preheat your Air Fryer to 160°C (320°F) for 5 minutes.
2. In a mixing bowl, beat together cream cheese and granulated sugar until smooth.
3. Add the egg and vanilla extract, and beat until well combined.
4. Stir in sour cream and flour until smooth.
5. Grease a mini muffin tin or line it with paper liners.
6. Spoon the cheesecake batter into the prepared muffin tin, filling each cup almost to the top.
7. Tap the muffin tin gently on the countertop to remove any air bubbles.
8. Place the muffin tin in the Air Fryer basket, ensuring there is space between each cheesecake bite.
9. Air fry at 160°C (320°F) for 25 minutes or until the cheesecake bites are set and slightly golden on top.
10. Once done, remove the cheesecake bites from the Air Fryer and let them cool in the muffin tin for 10 minutes.
11. Carefully remove the cheesecake bites from the muffin tin and transfer them to a wire rack to cool completely.
12. Chill the cheesecake bites in the refrigerator for at least 2 hours before serving.
13. Before serving, sprinkle graham cracker crumbs on top of each cheesecake bite.

Nutritional Info: Calories: 110 | Fat: 8g | Carbs: 7g | Protein: 2g

Air Fryer Function Used: Bake

Air Fryer Whoopie Pies

Prep: 20 mins | Cook: 10 mins | Serves: 12 whoopie pies

Ingredients:
- 200g (1 ½ cups) all-purpose flour
- 50g (⅓ cup) unsweetened cocoa powder
- 1 tsp baking soda
- Pinch of salt
- 100g (½ cup) unsalted butter, softened
- 150g (¾ cup) granulated sugar
- 1 large egg
- 1 tsp vanilla extract
- 120ml (½ cup) milk

Instructions:
1. Preheat your Air Fryer to 180°C (356°F) for 5 minutes.
2. In a mixing bowl, sift together flour, cocoa powder, baking soda, and salt.
3. In another bowl, cream together softened butter and granulated sugar until light and fluffy.
4. Add the egg and vanilla extract to the butter mixture, and beat until well combined.
5. Gradually add the dry ingredients to the wet ingredients, alternating with milk, and mix until smooth.
6. Spoon the batter into a piping bag fitted with a round tip.
7. Pipe small rounds of batter onto a parchment-lined baking sheet, spacing them apart.
8. Flatten the batter slightly with the back of a spoon to form whoopie pie shells.
9. Place the baking sheet in the Air Fryer basket, ensuring there is space between each whoopie pie.
10. Air fry at 180°C (356°F) for 10 minutes or until the whoopie pies are firm to the touch.
11. Once done, remove the whoopie pies from the Air Fryer and let them cool completely on the baking sheet.

Nutritional Info: Calories: 160 | Fat: 7g | Carbs: 22g | Protein: 2g

Air Fryer Function Used: Bake

Air Fryer Baked Doughnuts

Prep: 20 mins | Cook: 10 mins | Serves: 12 doughnuts

Ingredients:
- 250g (2 cups) all-purpose flour
- 100g (½ cup) granulated sugar
- 2 tsp baking powder
- ½ tsp salt
- 120ml (½ cup) milk
- 2 large eggs
- 60g (¼ cup) unsalted butter, melted
- 1 tsp vanilla extract
- Cooking spray or melted butter for greasing

Instructions:
- Preheat your Air Fryer to 180°C (356°F) for 5 minutes.
- In a mixing bowl, whisk together flour, sugar, baking powder, and salt.
- In another bowl, whisk together milk, eggs, melted butter, and vanilla extract.
- Pour the wet ingredients into the dry ingredients and mix until just combined.
- Grease the wells of a doughnut pan with cooking spray or melted butter.
- Spoon the batter into the prepared doughnut pan, filling each well about ¾ full.
- Place the doughnut pan in the Air Fryer basket, ensuring there is space between each doughnut.
- Air fry at 180°C (356°F) for 10 minutes or until the doughnuts are golden brown and cooked through.
- Once done, remove the doughnuts from the Air Fryer and let them cool in the pan for a few minutes.
- Carefully transfer the doughnuts to a wire rack to cool completely.
- Optionally, glaze or sprinkle the cooled doughnuts with your favorite toppings.

Nutritional Info: Calories: 180 | Fat: 6g | Carbs: 28g | Protein: 4g

Air Fryer Function Used: Bake

Air Fryer Profiteroles

Prep: 30 mins | Cook: 20 mins | Chill: 1 hour | Serves: 12 profiteroles

Ingredients:

For the Choux Pastry:

- 120ml (½ cup) water
- 60g (¼ cup) unsalted butter
- 1 tbsp granulated sugar
- Pinch of salt
- 70g (½ cup) all-purpose flour
- 2 large eggs

For the Filling:

- 250ml (1 cup) heavy cream
- 2 tbsp powdered sugar
- 1 tsp vanilla extract
- Chocolate sauce or powdered sugar for garnish

Instructions:

1. Preheat your Air Fryer to 200°C (392°F) for 5 minutes.
2. In a saucepan, combine water, butter, sugar, and salt. Bring to a boil over medium heat.
3. Reduce heat to low and add flour all at once. Stir vigorously until the mixture forms a ball and pulls away from the sides of the pan.
4. Remove from heat and let cool for 5 minutes.
5. Add eggs, one at a time, beating well after each addition until smooth.
6. Transfer the choux pastry dough to a piping bag fitted with a round tip.
7. Pipe small mounds onto a parchment-lined baking sheet, spacing them apart.
8. Place the baking sheet in the Air Fryer basket and air fry at 200°C (392°F) for 10 minutes.
9. Reduce temperature to 160°C (320°F) and continue to air fry for another 10 minutes or until the profiteroles are golden brown and puffed up.
10. Once done, remove the profiteroles from the Air Fryer and let them cool completely.
11. In a mixing bowl, beat heavy cream, powdered sugar, and vanilla extract until stiff peaks form.
12. Slice each profiterole in half horizontally and fill with whipped cream.
13. Drizzle with chocolate sauce or dust with powdered sugar before serving.

Nutritional Info: Calories: 180 | Fat: 14g | Carbs: 11g | Protein: 3g

CHAPTER SIX: FRUITY AND NUTTY DELIGHTS

Air Fryer Apple Cake

Prep: 15 mins | Cook: 40 mins | Serves: 8 slices

Ingredients:
- 2 large apples, peeled and diced
- 200g (1 cup) granulated sugar
- 2 large eggs
- 120ml (½ cup) vegetable oil
- 1 tsp vanilla extract
- 200g (1 ½ cups) all-purpose flour
- 1 tsp baking powder
- 1 tsp ground cinnamon
- Pinch of salt
- Powdered sugar for dusting

Instructions:
1. Preheat your Air Fryer to 160°C (320°F) for 5 minutes.
2. In a large bowl, mix diced apples and granulated sugar. Let it sit for 10 minutes.
3. Beat eggs, vegetable oil, and vanilla extract into the apple mixture.
4. In a separate bowl, sift together flour, baking powder, cinnamon, and salt.
5. Gradually add the dry ingredients to the wet ingredients, stirring until just combined.
6. Grease and flour a cake pan that fits inside your Air Fryer basket.
7. Pour the batter into the prepared pan, spreading it evenly.
8. Place the cake pan in the Air Fryer basket and air fry at 160°C (320°F) for 40 minutes or until a toothpick inserted into the center comes out clean.
9. Once done, remove the cake from the Air Fryer and let it cool in the pan for 10 minutes.
10. Transfer the cake to a wire rack to cool completely.
11. Dust the cooled cake with powdered sugar before serving.

Nutritional Info: Calories: 280 | Fat: 12g | Carbs: 40g | Protein: 4g

Air Fryer Function Used: Bake

Air Fryer Pear Cake

Prep: 20 mins | Cook: 45 mins | Serves: 8 slices

Ingredients:

- 2 ripe pears, peeled, cored, and sliced
- 150g (¾ cup) brown sugar
- 2 large eggs
- 120ml (½ cup) vegetable oil
- 1 tsp vanilla extract
- 200g (1 ½ cups) all-purpose flour
- 1 tsp baking powder
- ½ tsp ground ginger
- Pinch of salt
- Confectioners' sugar for garnish

Instructions:

1. Preheat your Air Fryer to 160°C (320°F) for 5 minutes.
2. In a bowl, mix sliced pears with brown sugar. Let it sit for 10 minutes.
3. Beat eggs, vegetable oil, and vanilla extract into the pear mixture.
4. In another bowl, sift together flour, baking powder, ground ginger, and salt.
5. Gradually add the dry ingredients to the wet ingredients, stirring until just combined.
6. Grease and flour a cake pan that fits inside your Air Fryer basket.
7. Pour the batter into the prepared pan, spreading it evenly.
8. Arrange the pear slices on top of the batter.
9. Place the cake pan in the Air Fryer basket and air fry at 160°C (320°F) for 45 minutes or until a toothpick inserted into the center comes out clean.
10. Once done, remove the cake from the Air Fryer and let it cool in the pan for 10 minutes.
11. Transfer the cake to a wire rack to cool completely.
12. Dust the cooled cake with confectioners' sugar before serving.

Nutritional Info: Calories: 290 | Fat: 13g | Carbs: 38g | Protein: 4g

Air Fryer Function Used: Bake

Air Fryer Pecan Pie Cake

Prep: 20 mins | Cook: 50 mins | Serves: 8 slices

Ingredients:

- 150g (¾ cup) unsalted butter, melted
- 150g (¾ cup) brown sugar
- 3 large eggs
- 1 tsp vanilla extract
- 200g (1 ½ cups) all-purpose flour
- 1 tsp baking powder
- ½ tsp ground cinnamon
- Pinch of salt
- 100g (1 cup) chopped pecans
- Maple syrup for drizzling

Instructions:

1. Preheat your Air Fryer to 160°C (320°F) for 5 minutes.
2. In a bowl, mix melted butter and brown sugar until well combined.
3. Beat in eggs, one at a time, followed by vanilla extract.
4. In another bowl, sift together flour, baking powder, ground cinnamon, and salt.
5. Gradually add the dry ingredients to the wet ingredients, stirring until just combined.
6. Fold in chopped pecans.
7. Grease and flour a cake pan that fits inside your Air Fryer basket.
8. Pour the batter into the prepared pan, spreading it evenly.
9. Place the cake pan in the Air Fryer basket and air fry at 160°C (320°F) for 50 minutes or until a toothpick inserted into the center comes out clean.
10. Once done, remove the cake from the Air Fryer and let it cool in the pan for 10 minutes.
11. Transfer the cake to a serving plate and drizzle with maple syrup before serving.

Nutritional Info: Calories: 320 | Fat: 18g | Carbs: 35g | Protein: 5g

Air Fryer Function Used: Bake

Air Fryer Walnut Cake

Prep: 20 mins | Cook: 45 mins | Serves: 8 slices

Ingredients:

- 150g (¾ cup) unsalted butter, softened
- 150g (¾ cup) granulated sugar
- 3 large eggs
- 1 tsp vanilla extract
- 200g (1 ½ cups) all-purpose flour
- 1 tsp baking powder
- Pinch of salt
- 100g (1 cup) chopped walnuts
- Honey for drizzling

Instructions:

1. Preheat your Air Fryer to 160°C (320°F) for 5 minutes.
2. In a bowl, cream together softened butter and granulated sugar until light and fluffy.
3. Beat in eggs, one at a time, followed by vanilla extract.
4. In another bowl, sift together flour, baking powder, and salt.
5. Gradually add the dry ingredients to the wet ingredients, stirring until just combined.
6. Fold in chopped walnuts.
7. Grease and flour a cake pan that fits inside your Air Fryer basket.
8. Pour the batter into the prepared pan, spreading it evenly.
9. Place the cake pan in the Air Fryer basket and air fry at 160°C (320°F) for 45 minutes or until a toothpick inserted into the center comes out clean.
10. Once done, remove the cake from the Air Fryer and let it cool in the pan for 10 minutes.
11. Transfer the cake to a serving plate and drizzle with honey before serving.

Nutritional Info: Calories: 290 | Fat: 16g | Carbs: 33g | Protein: 5g

Air Fryer Function Used: Bake

Air Fryer Pistachio Cake

Prep: 20 mins | Cook: 50 mins | Serves: 8 slices

Ingredients:
- 150g (¾ cup) unsalted butter, softened
- 150g (¾ cup) granulated sugar
- 3 large eggs
- 1 tsp vanilla extract
- 200g (1 ½ cups) all-purpose flour
- 1 tsp baking powder
- Pinch of salt
- 100g (1 cup) shelled pistachios, chopped
- Pistachio glaze (optional):
- 100g (1 cup) powdered sugar
- 2-3 tbsp milk
- ¼ tsp pistachio extract

Instructions:
1. Preheat your Air Fryer to 160°C (320°F) for 5 minutes.
2. In a bowl, cream together softened butter and granulated sugar until light and fluffy.
3. Beat in eggs, one at a time, followed by vanilla extract.
4. In another bowl, sift together flour, baking powder, and salt.
5. Gradually add the dry ingredients to the wet ingredients, stirring until just combined.
6. Fold in chopped pistachios.
7. Grease and flour a cake pan that fits inside your Air Fryer basket.
8. Pour the batter into the prepared pan, spreading it evenly.
9. Place the cake pan in the Air Fryer basket and air fry at 160°C (320°F) for 50 minutes or until a toothpick inserted into the center comes out clean.
10. Once done, remove the cake from the Air Fryer and let it cool in the pan for 10 minutes.
11. Transfer the cake to a wire rack set over a baking sheet.
12. If desired, prepare the pistachio glaze by mixing powdered sugar, milk, and pistachio extract until smooth. Drizzle the glaze over the cooled cake.
13. Let the glaze set before slicing and serving.

Nutritional Info: Calories: 320 | Fat: 16g | Carbs: 40g | Protein: 5g

Air Fryer Function Used: Bake

Air Fryer Lemon Raspberry Cake

Prep: 20 mins | Cook: 45 mins | Serves: 8 slices

Ingredients:

- 150g (¾ cup) unsalted butter, softened
- 150g (¾ cup) granulated sugar
- 3 large eggs
- 1 tsp vanilla extract
- 200g (1 ½ cups) all-purpose flour
- 1 tsp baking powder
- Pinch of salt
- Zest of 1 lemon
- 120g (1 cup) fresh raspberries

Instructions:

1. Preheat your Air Fryer to 160°C (320°F) for 5 minutes.
2. In a bowl, cream together softened butter and granulated sugar until light and fluffy.
3. Beat in eggs, one at a time, followed by vanilla extract.
4. In another bowl, sift together flour, baking powder, and salt.
5. Gradually add the dry ingredients to the wet ingredients, stirring until just combined.
6. Fold in lemon zest and fresh raspberries.
7. Grease and flour a cake pan that fits inside your Air Fryer basket.
8. Pour the batter into the prepared pan, spreading it evenly.
9. Place the cake pan in the Air Fryer basket and air fry at 160°C (320°F) for 45 minutes or until a toothpick inserted into the center comes out clean.
10. Once done, remove the cake from the Air Fryer and let it cool in the pan for 10 minutes.
11. Transfer the cake to a wire rack to cool completely before slicing and serving.

Nutritional Info: Calories: 280 | Fat: 14g | Carbs: 35g | Protein: 5g

Air Fryer Function Used: Bake

Air Fryer Strawberry Shortcake

Prep: 20 mins | Cook: 25 mins | Serves: 6 servings

Ingredients:

- 200g (1 ½ cups) all-purpose flour
- 50g (¼ cup) granulated sugar
- 1 tbsp baking powder
- Pinch of salt
- 85g (6 tbsp) unsalted butter, cold and cubed
- 120ml (½ cup) milk
- 1 large egg
- 1 tsp vanilla extract
- 250g (1 ½ cups) fresh strawberries, sliced
- Whipped cream for serving

Instructions:

1. Preheat your Air Fryer to 160°C (320°F) for 5 minutes.
2. In a large bowl, combine flour, sugar, baking powder, and salt.
3. Add cold cubed butter to the flour mixture and use your fingers or a pastry cutter to cut the butter into the flour until it resembles coarse crumbs.
4. In a separate bowl, whisk together milk, egg, and vanilla extract.
5. Pour the wet ingredients into the dry ingredients and stir until just combined. Do not overmix.
6. Turn the dough out onto a lightly floured surface and gently knead it a few times until it comes together.
7. Pat the dough into a circle about 1-inch thick. Use a biscuit cutter or a glass to cut out circles of dough.
8. Place the dough circles in the Air Fryer basket, leaving space between each one.
9. Air fry at 160°C (320°F) for 12-15 minutes or until the shortcakes are golden brown and cooked through.
10. Once done, remove the shortcakes from the Air Fryer and let them cool slightly.
11. To serve, split the shortcakes in half horizontally. Top each bottom half with sliced strawberries and a dollop of whipped cream. Place the other half of the shortcake on top.
12. Serve immediately.

Nutritional Info: Calories: 280 | Fat: 11g | Carbs: 39g | Protein: 5g

Air Fryer Function Used: Bake

Air Fryer Cherry Cake

Prep: 20 mins | Cook: 40 mins | Serves: 8 slices

Ingredients:
- 200g (1 ½ cups) all-purpose flour
- 150g (¾ cup) granulated sugar
- 1 tsp baking powder
- Pinch of salt
- 85g (6 tbsp) unsalted butter, softened
- 120ml (½ cup) milk
- 2 large eggs
- 1 tsp almond extract
- 200g (1 ½ cups) fresh cherries, pitted and halved

Instructions:
1. Preheat your Air Fryer to 160°C (320°F) for 5 minutes.
2. In a large bowl, whisk together flour, sugar, baking powder, and salt.
3. Add softened butter to the flour mixture and mix until crumbly.
4. In a separate bowl, whisk together milk, eggs, and almond extract.
5. Pour the wet ingredients into the dry ingredients and mix until just combined.
6. Gently fold in the halved cherries.
7. Grease and flour a cake pan that fits inside your Air Fryer basket.
8. Pour the batter into the prepared pan, spreading it evenly.
9. Place the cake pan in the Air Fryer basket and air fry at 160°C (320°F) for 40 minutes or until a toothpick inserted into the center comes out clean.
10. Once done, remove the cake from the Air Fryer and let it cool in the pan for 10 minutes.
11. Transfer the cake to a wire rack to cool completely before slicing and serving.

Nutritional Info: Calories: 240 | Fat: 9g | Carbs: 35g | Protein: 4g

Air Fryer Function Used: Bake

Air Fryer Pineapple Upside-Down Cake

Prep: 20 mins | Cook: 30 mins | Serves: 8 slices

Ingredients:

For the Pineapple Topping:

- 50g (¼ cup) unsalted butter
- 100g (½ cup) brown sugar
- 6 pineapple rings, canned or fresh

For the Cake Batter:

- 150g (¾ cup) granulated sugar
- 2 large eggs
- 1 tsp vanilla extract
- 120ml (½ cup) pineapple juice
- 120ml (½ cup) vegetable oil
- 200g (1 ½ cups) all-purpose flour
- 1 tsp baking powder
- Pinch of salt
- Maraschino cherries for garnish

Instructions:

1. Preheat your Air Fryer to 160°C (320°F) for 5 minutes.
2. In a small saucepan, melt butter over low heat. Add brown sugar and stir until dissolved.
3. Pour the butter and sugar mixture into the bottom of a greased and floured cake pan that fits inside your Air Fryer basket.
4. Arrange pineapple rings on top of the sugar mixture in the cake pan.
5. In a large bowl, whisk together granulated sugar, eggs, vanilla extract, pineapple juice, and vegetable oil until well combined.
6. In another bowl, sift together flour, baking powder, and salt.
7. Gradually add the dry ingredients to the wet ingredients, stirring until just combined.
8. Pour the cake batter over the pineapple rings in the cake pan, spreading it evenly.
9. Place the cake pan in the Air Fryer basket and air fry at 160°C (320°F) for 30 minutes or until a toothpick inserted into the center comes out clean.
10. Once done, remove the cake from the Air Fryer and let it cool in the pan for 10 minutes.
11. Carefully invert the cake onto a serving plate. If any pineapple slices stick to the pan, gently remove them and place them back onto the cake.
12. Garnish the cake with maraschino cherries before serving.

Nutritional Info: Calories: 280 | Fat: 12g | Carbs: 40g | Protein: 3g

Air Fryer Function Used: Bake

Air Fryer Tropical Fruit Cake

Prep: 20 mins | Cook: 40 mins | Serves: 8 slices

Ingredients:

- 200g (1 ½ cups) all-purpose flour
- 150g (¾ cup) granulated sugar
- 1 tsp baking powder
- Pinch of salt
- 85g (6 tbsp) unsalted butter, softened
- 120ml (½ cup) coconut milk
- 2 large eggs
- 1 tsp vanilla extract
- 100g (½ cup) diced tropical fruits (such as mango, pineapple, and papaya)
- 50g (½ cup) shredded coconut

Instructions:

1. Preheat your Air Fryer to 160°C (320°F) for 5 minutes.
2. In a large bowl, whisk together flour, sugar, baking powder, and salt.
3. Add softened butter to the flour mixture and mix until crumbly.
4. In a separate bowl, whisk together coconut milk, eggs, and vanilla extract.
5. Pour the wet ingredients into the dry ingredients and mix until just combined.
6. Fold in diced tropical fruits and shredded coconut.
7. Grease and flour a cake pan that fits inside your Air Fryer basket.
8. Pour the batter into the prepared pan, spreading it evenly.
9. Place the cake pan in the Air Fryer basket and air fry at 160°C (320°F) for 40 minutes or until a toothpick inserted into the center comes out clean.
10. Once done, remove the cake from the Air Fryer and let it cool in the pan for 10 minutes.
11. Transfer the cake to a wire rack to cool completely before slicing and serving.

Nutritional Info: Calories: 260 | Fat: 11g | Carbs: 35g | Protein: 4g

Air Fryer Function Used: Bake

Air Fryer Cranberry Orange Cake

Prep: 20 mins | Cook: 40 mins | Serves: 8 slices

Ingredients:

- 200g (1 ½ cups) all-purpose flour
- 150g (¾ cup) granulated sugar
- 1 tsp baking powder
- ½ tsp baking soda
- Pinch of salt
- Zest of 1 orange
- 120ml (½ cup) orange juice
- 85g (6 tbsp) unsalted butter, melted
- 2 large eggs
- 1 tsp vanilla extract
- 100g (1 cup) fresh cranberries
- Powdered sugar for dusting

Instructions:

1. Preheat your Air Fryer to 160°C (320°F) for 5 minutes.
2. In a large bowl, whisk together flour, sugar, baking powder, baking soda, and salt.
3. Add orange zest, orange juice, melted butter, eggs, and vanilla extract to the dry ingredients. Mix until just combined.
4. Gently fold in fresh cranberries.
5. Grease and flour a cake pan that fits inside your Air Fryer basket.
6. Pour the batter into the prepared pan, spreading it evenly.
7. Place the cake pan in the Air Fryer basket and air fry at 160°C (320°F) for 40 minutes or until a toothpick inserted into the center comes out clean.
8. Once done, remove the cake from the Air Fryer and let it cool in the pan for 10 minutes.
9. Transfer the cake to a wire rack to cool completely.
10. Dust the cooled cake with powdered sugar before serving.

Nutritional Info: Calories: 270 | Fat: 9g | Carbs: 42g | Protein: 4g

Air Fryer Function Used: Bake

Air Fryer Blueberry Buckle

Prep: 20 mins | Cook: 40 mins | Serves: 8 slices

Ingredients:

- 200g (1 ½ cups) all-purpose flour
- 150g (¾ cup) granulated sugar
- 1 tsp baking powder
- Pinch of salt
- 85g (6 tbsp) unsalted butter, softened
- 120ml (½ cup) milk
- 1 large egg
- 1 tsp vanilla extract
- 200g (1 ½ cups) fresh blueberries
- Streusel topping:
- 50g (¼ cup) granulated sugar
- 50g (¼ cup) all-purpose flour
- 30g (2 tbsp) unsalted butter, melted
- ½ tsp ground cinnamon

Instructions:

1. Preheat your Air Fryer to 160°C (320°F) for 5 minutes.
2. In a large bowl, whisk together flour, sugar, baking powder, and salt.
3. Add softened butter to the flour mixture and mix until crumbly.
4. In a separate bowl, whisk together milk, egg, and vanilla extract.
5. Pour the wet ingredients into the dry ingredients and mix until just combined.
6. Gently fold in fresh blueberries.
7. Grease and flour a cake pan that fits inside your Air Fryer basket.
8. Pour the batter into the prepared pan, spreading it evenly.
9. In a small bowl, prepare the streusel topping by mixing sugar, flour, melted butter, and ground cinnamon until crumbly.
10. Sprinkle the streusel topping evenly over the batter.
11. Place the cake pan in the Air Fryer basket and air fry at 160°C (320°F) for 40 minutes or until a toothpick inserted into the center comes out clean.
12. Once done, remove the cake from the Air Fryer and let it cool in the pan for 10 minutes.
13. Transfer the cake to a wire rack to cool completely before slicing and serving.

Nutritional Info: Calories: 290 | Fat: 11g | Carbs: 44g | Protein: 4g

Air Fryer Function Used: Bake

Air Fryer Apricot Almond Cake

Prep: 20 mins | Cook: 40 mins | Serves: 8 slices

Ingredients:
- 200g (1 ½ cups) all-purpose flour
- 150g (¾ cup) granulated sugar
- 1 tsp baking powder
- Pinch of salt
- 85g (6 tbsp) unsalted butter, softened
- 120ml (½ cup) milk
- 2 large eggs
- 1 tsp almond extract
- 100g (¾ cup) dried apricots, chopped
- 50g (½ cup) almond flakes

Instructions:
1. Preheat your Air Fryer to 160°C (320°F) for 5 minutes.
2. In a large bowl, whisk together flour, sugar, baking powder, and salt.
3. Add softened butter to the flour mixture and mix until crumbly.
4. In a separate bowl, whisk together milk, eggs, and almond extract.
5. Pour the wet ingredients into the dry ingredients and mix until just combined.
6. Gently fold in chopped dried apricots.
7. Grease and flour a cake pan that fits inside your Air Fryer basket.
8. Pour the batter into the prepared pan, spreading it evenly.
9. Sprinkle almond flakes over the top of the batter.
10. Place the cake pan in the Air Fryer basket and air fry at 160°C (320°F) for 40 minutes or until a toothpick inserted into the center comes out clean.
11. Once done, remove the cake from the Air Fryer and let it cool in the pan for 10 minutes.
12. Transfer the cake to a wire rack to cool completely before slicing and serving.

Nutritional Info: Calories: 270 | Fat: 10g | Carbs: 40g | Protein: 5g

Air Fryer Function Used: Bake

Air Fryer Fig and Walnut Cake

Prep: 20 mins | Cook: 45 mins | Serves: 8 slices

Ingredients:

- 200g (1 ½ cups) all-purpose flour
- 150g (¾ cup) granulated sugar
- 1 tsp baking powder
- Pinch of salt
- 85g (6 tbsp) unsalted butter, softened
- 120ml (½ cup) milk
- 2 large eggs
- 1 tsp vanilla extract
- 100g (¾ cup) dried figs, chopped
- 50g (½ cup) walnuts, chopped

Instructions:

1. Preheat your Air Fryer to 160°C (320°F) for 5 minutes.
2. In a large bowl, whisk together flour, sugar, baking powder, and salt.
3. Add softened butter to the flour mixture and mix until crumbly.
4. In a separate bowl, whisk together milk, eggs, and vanilla extract.
5. Pour the wet ingredients into the dry ingredients and mix until just combined.
6. Gently fold in chopped dried figs and walnuts.
7. Grease and flour a cake pan that fits inside your Air Fryer basket.
8. Pour the batter into the prepared pan, spreading it evenly.
9. Place the cake pan in the Air Fryer basket and air fry at 160°C (320°F) for 45 minutes or until a toothpick inserted into the center comes out clean.
10. Once done, remove the cake from the Air Fryer and let it cool in the pan for 10 minutes.
11. Transfer the cake to a wire rack to cool completely before slicing and serving.

Nutritional Info: Calories: 280 | Fat: 11g | Carbs: 40g | Protein: 5g

Air Fryer Function Used: Bake

Air Fryer Mango Upside-Down Cake

Prep: 20 mins | Cook: 40 mins | Serves: 8 slices

Ingredients:
For the Mango Topping:

- 50g (¼ cup) unsalted butter
- 100g (½ cup) brown sugar
- 2 ripe mangoes, peeled and sliced

For the Cake Batter:

- 200g (1 ½ cups) all-purpose flour
- 150g (¾ cup) granulated sugar
- 1 tsp baking powder
- Pinch of salt
- 85g (6 tbsp) unsalted butter, softened
- 120ml (½ cup) milk
- 2 large eggs
- 1 tsp vanilla extract

Instructions:
1. Preheat your Air Fryer to 160°C (320°F) for 5 minutes.
2. In a small saucepan, melt butter over low heat. Add brown sugar and stir until dissolved.
3. Pour the butter and sugar mixture into the bottom of a greased and floured cake pan that fits inside your Air Fryer basket.
4. Arrange mango slices on top of the sugar mixture in the cake pan.
5. In a large bowl, whisk together flour, sugar, baking powder, and salt.
6. Add softened butter to the flour mixture and mix until crumbly.
7. In a separate bowl, whisk together milk, eggs, and vanilla extract.
8. Pour the wet ingredients into the dry ingredients and mix until just combined.
9. Pour the cake batter over the mango slices in the cake pan, spreading it evenly.
10. Place the cake pan in the Air Fryer basket and air fry at 160°C (320°F) for 40 minutes or until a toothpick inserted into the center comes out clean.
11. Once done, remove the cake from the Air Fryer and let it cool in the pan for 10 minutes.
12. Carefully invert the cake onto a serving plate. If any mango slices stick to the pan, gently remove them and place them back onto the cake.
13. Serve warm or at room temperature.

Nutritional Info: Calories: 290 | Fat: 12g | Carbs: 42g | Protein: 4g

Air Fryer Function Used: Bake

Air Fryer Pecan Praline Cake

Prep: 20 mins | Cook: 45 mins | Serves: 8 slices

Ingredients:
- 200g (1 ½ cups) all-purpose flour
- 150g (¾ cup) granulated sugar
- 1 tsp baking powder
- Pinch of salt
- 85g (6 tbsp) unsalted butter, softened
- 120ml (½ cup) milk
- 2 large eggs
- 1 tsp vanilla extract
- 100g (¾ cup) chopped pecans
- 50g (¼ cup) brown sugar
- 30g (2 tbsp) unsalted butter, melted

Instructions:
1. Preheat your Air Fryer to 160°C (320°F) for 5 minutes.
2. In a small bowl, mix together chopped pecans, brown sugar, and melted butter to make the praline topping.
3. Grease and flour a cake pan that fits inside your Air Fryer basket.
4. Spread the praline topping evenly on the bottom of the prepared cake pan.
5. In a large bowl, whisk together flour, sugar, baking powder, and salt.
6. Add softened butter to the flour mixture and mix until crumbly.
7. In a separate bowl, whisk together milk, eggs, and vanilla extract.
8. Pour the wet ingredients into the dry ingredients and mix until just combined.
9. Gently fold in chopped pecans.
10. Pour the cake batter over the praline topping in the cake pan, spreading it evenly.
11. Place the cake pan in the Air Fryer basket and air fry at 160°C (320°F) for 45 minutes or until a toothpick inserted into the center comes out clean.
12. Once done, remove the cake from the Air Fryer and let it cool in the pan for 10 minutes.

13. Carefully invert the cake onto a serving plate. If any praline topping sticks to the pan, gently remove it and place it back onto the cake.
14. Serve warm or at room temperature.

Nutritional Info: Calories: 300 | Fat: 13g | Carbs: 40g | Protein: 5g

Air Fryer Function Used: Bake

CHAPTER SEVEN: CHEESECAKE AND MOUSSE MARVELS

Air Fryer Classic Cheesecake

Prep: 15 mins | Cook: 40 mins | Chill: 4 hours | Serves: 8 slices

Ingredients:
- 200g (2 cups) digestive biscuits/graham crackers, crushed
- 100g (7 tbsp) unsalted butter, melted
- 500g (2 cups) cream cheese, softened
- 200g (1 cup) granulated sugar
- 3 large eggs
- 1 tsp vanilla extract
- 120ml (½ cup) sour cream
- 1 tbsp all-purpose flour
- Pinch of salt

Instructions:
1. Preheat your Air Fryer to 160°C (320°F) for 5 minutes.
2. In a bowl, mix crushed biscuits/graham crackers and melted butter until well combined. Press mixture into the bottom of a greased springform pan.
3. In another bowl, beat cream cheese until smooth. Gradually add sugar and beat until creamy.
4. Add eggs, one at a time, mixing well after each addition. Stir in vanilla extract, sour cream, flour, and salt until smooth.
5. Pour cream cheese mixture over the prepared crust in the springform pan.
6. Place the pan in the Air Fryer basket and air fry at 160°C (320°F) for 40 minutes or until the edges are set and the center is slightly jiggly.
7. Once done, turn off the Air Fryer and let the cheesecake cool in the basket for 10 minutes with the door slightly open.
8. Remove the cheesecake from the Air Fryer and let it cool completely on a wire rack.
9. Chill the cheesecake in the refrigerator for at least 4 hours or overnight before slicing and serving.

Nutritional Info: Calories: 380 | Fat: 26g | Carbs: 30g | Protein: 6g

Air Fryer Function Used: Bake

Air Fryer Strawberry Cheesecake

Prep: 20 mins | Cook: 40 mins | Chill: 4 hours | Serves: 8 slices

Ingredients:

- 200g (2 cups) digestive biscuits/graham crackers, crushed
- 100g (7 tbsp) unsalted butter, melted
- 500g (2 cups) cream cheese, softened
- 200g (1 cup) granulated sugar
- 3 large eggs
- 1 tsp vanilla extract
- 120ml (½ cup) sour cream
- 1 tbsp all-purpose flour
- Pinch of salt
- 200g (1 ½ cups) fresh strawberries, sliced

- ### *Instructions:*
- Preheat your Air Fryer to 160°C (320°F) for 5 minutes.
- In a bowl, mix crushed biscuits/graham crackers and melted butter until well combined. Press mixture into the bottom of a greased springform pan.
- In another bowl, beat cream cheese until smooth. Gradually add sugar and beat until creamy.
- Add eggs, one at a time, mixing well after each addition. Stir in vanilla extract, sour cream, flour, and salt until smooth.
- Pour cream cheese mixture over the prepared crust in the springform pan.
- Arrange sliced strawberries on top of the cream cheese mixture.
- Place the pan in the Air Fryer basket and air fry at 160°C (320°F) for 40 minutes or until the edges are set and the center is slightly jiggly.
- Once done, turn off the Air Fryer and let the cheesecake cool in the basket for 10 minutes with the door slightly open.
- Remove the cheesecake from the Air Fryer and let it cool completely on a wire rack.
- Chill the cheesecake in the refrigerator for at least 4 hours or overnight before slicing and serving.

Nutritional Info: Calories: 400 | Fat: 27g | Carbs: 32g | Protein: 7g

Air Fryer Function Used: Bake

Air Fryer Chocolate Cheesecake

Prep: 20 mins | Cook: 40 mins | Chill: 4 hours | Serves: 8 slices

Ingredients:

- 200g (2 cups) chocolate biscuits, crushed
- 100g (7 tbsp) unsalted butter, melted
- 500g (2 cups) cream cheese, softened
- 200g (1 cup) granulated sugar
- 3 large eggs
- 1 tsp vanilla extract
- 120ml (½ cup) sour cream
- 1 tbsp all-purpose flour
- Pinch of salt
- 150g (1 cup) semisweet chocolate chips, melted

Instructions:

1. Preheat your Air Fryer to 160°C (320°F) for 5 minutes.
2. In a bowl, mix crushed chocolate biscuits and melted butter until well combined. Press mixture into the bottom of a greased springform pan.
3. In another bowl, beat cream cheese until smooth. Gradually add sugar and beat until creamy.
4. Add eggs, one at a time, mixing well after each addition. Stir in vanilla extract, sour cream, flour, and salt until smooth.
5. Stir in melted chocolate until fully incorporated into the cream cheese mixture.
6. Pour cream cheese mixture over the prepared crust in the springform pan.
7. Place the pan in the Air Fryer basket and air fry at 160°C (320°F) for 40 minutes or until the edges are set and the center is slightly jiggly.
8. Once done, turn off the Air Fryer and let the cheesecake cool in the basket for 10 minutes with the door slightly open.
9. Remove the cheesecake from the Air Fryer and let it cool completely on a wire rack.

10. Chill the cheesecake in the refrigerator for at least 4 hours or overnight before slicing and serving.

Nutritional Info: Calories: 420 | Fat: 30g | Carbs: 33g | Protein: 7g

Air Fryer Function Used: Bake

Air Fryer Lemon Cheesecake

Prep: 20 mins | Cook: 40 mins | Chill: 4 hours | Serves: 8 slices

Ingredients:

- 200g (2 cups) digestive biscuits/graham crackers, crushed
- 100g (7 tbsp) unsalted butter, melted
- 500g (2 cups) cream cheese, softened
- 200g (1 cup) granulated sugar
- 3 large eggs
- 1 tsp vanilla extract
- 120ml (½ cup) sour cream
- 1 tbsp all-purpose flour
- Pinch of salt
- Zest of 2 lemons
- 2 tbsp fresh lemon juice

Instructions:

1. Preheat your Air Fryer to 160°C (320°F) for 5 minutes.
2. In a bowl, mix crushed biscuits/graham crackers and melted butter until well combined. Press mixture into the bottom of a greased springform pan.
3. In another bowl, beat cream cheese until smooth. Gradually add sugar and beat until creamy.
4. Add eggs, one at a time, mixing well after each addition. Stir in vanilla extract, sour cream, flour, and salt until smooth.
5. Stir in lemon zest and lemon juice until fully incorporated into the cream cheese mixture.
6. Pour cream cheese mixture over the prepared crust in the springform pan.
7. Place the pan in the Air Fryer basket and air fry at 160°C (320°F) for 40 minutes or until the edges are set and the center is slightly jiggly.

8. Once done, turn off the Air Fryer and let the cheesecake cool in the basket for 10 minutes with the door slightly open.
9. Remove the cheesecake from the Air Fryer and let it cool completely on a wire rack.
10. Chill the cheesecake in the refrigerator for at least 4 hours or overnight before slicing and serving.

Nutritional Info: Calories: 380 | Fat: 27g | Carbs: 31g | Protein: 6g

Air Fryer Function Used: Bake

Air Fryer Oreo Cheesecake

Prep: 20 mins | Cook: 40 mins | Chill: 4 hours | Serves: 8 slices

Ingredients:
- 200g (2 cups) Oreo cookies, crushed
- 100g (7 tbsp) unsalted butter, melted
- 500g (2 cups) cream cheese, softened
- 200g (1 cup) granulated sugar
- 3 large eggs
- 1 tsp vanilla extract
- 120ml (½ cup) sour cream
- 1 tbsp all-purpose flour
- Pinch of salt

Instructions:
1. Preheat your Air Fryer to 160°C (320°F) for 5 minutes.
2. In a bowl, mix crushed Oreo cookies and melted butter until well combined. Press mixture into the bottom of a greased springform pan.
3. In another bowl, beat cream cheese until smooth. Gradually add sugar and beat until creamy.
4. Add eggs, one at a time, mixing well after each addition. Stir in vanilla extract, sour cream, flour, and salt until smooth.
5. Pour cream cheese mixture over the prepared Oreo crust in the springform pan.
6. Place the pan in the Air Fryer basket and air fry at 160°C (320°F) for 40 minutes or until the edges are set and the center is slightly jiggly.

7. Once done, turn off the Air Fryer and let the cheesecake cool in the basket for 10 minutes with the door slightly open.
8. Remove the cheesecake from the Air Fryer and let it cool completely on a wire rack.
9. Chill the cheesecake in the refrigerator for at least 4 hours or overnight before slicing and serving.

Nutritional Info: Calories: 420 | Fat: 29g | Carbs: 36g | Protein: 7g

Air Fryer Function Used: Bake

Air Fryer Chocolate Mousse Cake

Prep: 20 mins | Chill: 4 hours | Serves: 8 slices

Ingredients:
- 200g (7 oz) dark chocolate, chopped
- 100g (½ cup) unsalted butter
- 4 large eggs, separated
- 50g (¼ cup) granulated sugar
- 240ml (1 cup) heavy cream
- 1 tsp vanilla extract

Instructions:
1. In a heatproof bowl, melt the dark chocolate and unsalted butter together over a saucepan of simmering water. Let it cool slightly.
2. In another bowl, beat egg yolks and sugar until pale and fluffy. Stir in the melted chocolate mixture and vanilla extract until well combined.
3. In a separate bowl, whip the heavy cream until stiff peaks form.
4. Gently fold the whipped cream into the chocolate mixture until smooth.
5. In another clean bowl, beat egg whites until stiff peaks form.
6. Carefully fold the beaten egg whites into the chocolate mixture until no streaks remain.
7. Pour the mousse mixture into a greased and lined cake pan that fits inside the Air Fryer basket.
8. Chill the mousse cake in the refrigerator for at least 4 hours or until set.
9. Once set, remove the mousse cake from the pan, slice, and serve chilled.

Nutritional Info: Calories: 320 | Fat: 25g | Carbs: 18g | Protein: 6g

Air Fryer Function Used: None (No baking required)

Air Fryer Raspberry Mousse Cake

Prep: 20 mins | Chill: 4 hours | Serves: 8 slices

Ingredients:

- 200g (7 oz) white chocolate, chopped
- 240ml (1 cup) heavy cream
- 200g (1 ½ cups) fresh raspberries
- 2 tbsp granulated sugar
- 4 large eggs, separated
- 1 tsp vanilla extract

Instructions:

1. In a heatproof bowl, melt the white chocolate over a saucepan of simmering water. Let it cool slightly.
2. In a blender, puree the fresh raspberries with granulated sugar until smooth. Strain the puree to remove seeds.
3. In a bowl, beat egg yolks and vanilla extract until pale and fluffy. Gradually pour in the raspberry puree, mixing well.
4. Stir in the melted white chocolate until well combined.
5. In a separate bowl, whip the heavy cream until stiff peaks form.
6. Gently fold the whipped cream into the raspberry mixture until smooth.
7. In another clean bowl, beat egg whites until stiff peaks form.
8. Carefully fold the beaten egg whites into the raspberry mixture until no streaks remain.
9. Pour the mousse mixture into a greased and lined cake pan that fits inside the Air Fryer basket.
10. Chill the mousse cake in the refrigerator for at least 4 hours or until set.
11. Once set, remove the mousse cake from the pan, slice, and serve chilled.

Nutritional Info: Calories: 280 | Fat: 20g | Carbs: 21g | Protein: 6g

Air Fryer Function Used: None (No baking required)

Air Fryer Lemon Mousse Cake

Prep: 20 mins | Chill: 4 hours | Serves: 8 slices

Ingredients:

- 200g (7 oz) white chocolate, chopped
- 240ml (1 cup) heavy cream
- Zest of 2 lemons
- 120ml (½ cup) fresh lemon juice
- 2 tbsp granulated sugar
- 4 large eggs, separated
- 1 tsp vanilla extract

Instructions:

1. In a heatproof bowl, melt the white chocolate over a saucepan of simmering water. Let it cool slightly.
2. In a bowl, beat egg yolks, lemon zest, lemon juice, and granulated sugar until pale and fluffy.
3. Stir in the melted white chocolate until well combined.
4. In a separate bowl, whip the heavy cream until stiff peaks form.
5. Gently fold the whipped cream into the lemon mixture until smooth.
6. In another clean bowl, beat egg whites until stiff peaks form.
7. Carefully fold the beaten egg whites into the lemon mixture until no streaks remain.
8. Pour the mousse mixture into a greased and lined cake pan that fits inside the Air Fryer basket.
9. Chill the mousse cake in the refrigerator for at least 4 hours or until set.
10. Once set, remove the mousse cake from the pan, slice, and serve chilled.

Nutritional Info: Calories: 290 | Fat: 21g | Carbs: 22g | Protein: 6g

Air Fryer Function Used: None (No baking required)

Air Fryer Tiramisu Cake

Prep: 30 mins | Chill: 4 hours | Serves: 8 slices

Ingredients:
- 250g (1 cup) mascarpone cheese
- 120ml (½ cup) heavy cream
- 3 large eggs, separated
- 100g (½ cup) granulated sugar
- 1 tsp vanilla extract
- 200ml (¾ cup) strong brewed coffee, cooled
- 2 tbsp coffee liqueur (optional)
- 200g (7 oz) ladyfinger biscuits
- Cocoa powder, for dusting

Instructions:
1. In a mixing bowl, beat mascarpone cheese until smooth.
2. In a separate bowl, whip the heavy cream until stiff peaks form.
3. In another bowl, beat egg yolks with sugar and vanilla extract until pale and fluffy.
4. Gradually fold the whipped cream into the mascarpone mixture until smooth.
5. In another clean bowl, beat egg whites until stiff peaks form.
6. Gently fold the beaten egg whites into the mascarpone mixture until no streaks remain.
7. Mix the cooled coffee with coffee liqueur (if using) in a shallow dish.
8. Quickly dip each ladyfinger biscuit into the coffee mixture, ensuring they are soaked but not soggy.
9. Arrange a layer of soaked ladyfinger biscuits in the bottom of a greased and lined cake pan that fits inside the Air Fryer basket.
10. Spread half of the mascarpone mixture over the ladyfinger layer.
11. Repeat with another layer of soaked ladyfinger biscuits and remaining mascarpone mixture.
12. Cover the cake pan with plastic wrap and chill the tiramisu cake in the refrigerator for at least 4 hours or overnight.
13. Once set, dust the top of the tiramisu cake with cocoa powder before slicing and serving.

Nutritional Info: Calories: 290 | Fat: 20g | Carbs: 23g | Protein: 5g

Air Fryer Function Used: None (No baking required)

Air Fryer Peanut Butter Mousse Cake

Prep: 20 mins | Chill: 4 hours | Serves: 8 slices

Ingredients:
- 200g (7 oz) milk chocolate, chopped
- 240ml (1 cup) heavy cream
- 150g (½ cup) creamy peanut butter
- 2 tbsp powdered sugar
- 2 tsp gelatin powder
- 2 tbsp cold water
- 2 tbsp hot water

Instructions:
1. In a heatproof bowl, melt the milk chocolate over a saucepan of simmering water. Let it cool slightly.
2. In another bowl, beat heavy cream until stiff peaks form.
3. In a separate bowl, mix peanut butter and powdered sugar until smooth.
4. Stir the melted chocolate into the peanut butter mixture until well combined.
5. In a small bowl, sprinkle gelatin over cold water and let it sit for 5 minutes to bloom.
6. Stir in hot water to dissolve the gelatin completely.
7. Fold the whipped cream into the peanut butter-chocolate mixture until smooth.
8. Add the dissolved gelatin mixture to the mousse mixture and fold gently until smooth.
9. Pour the peanut butter mousse mixture into a greased and lined cake pan that fits inside the Air Fryer basket.
10. Chill the mousse cake in the refrigerator for at least 4 hours or until set.
11. Once set, remove the mousse cake from the pan, slice, and serve chilled.

Nutritional Info: Calories: 350 | Fat: 26g | Carbs: 25g | Protein: 7g

Air Fryer Function Used: None (No baking required)

Air Fryer Mango Mousse Cake

Prep: 20 mins | Chill: 4 hours | Serves: 8 slices

Ingredients:
- 2 large ripe mangoes, peeled and diced
- 200ml (¾ cup) heavy cream
- 100g (½ cup) granulated sugar
- 2 tsp gelatin powder
- 2 tbsp cold water
- 2 tbsp hot water

Instructions:
1. Puree the diced mangoes in a blender until smooth. Set aside.
2. In a small bowl, sprinkle gelatin over cold water and let it sit for 5 minutes to bloom.
3. Stir in hot water to dissolve the gelatin completely.
4. In a mixing bowl, whip the heavy cream until stiff peaks form.
5. Gently fold the mango puree into the whipped cream until well combined.
6. Add the dissolved gelatin mixture to the mango mousse mixture and fold gently until smooth.
7. Pour the mango mousse mixture into a greased and lined cake pan that fits inside the Air Fryer basket.
8. Chill the mousse cake in the refrigerator for at least 4 hours or until set.
9. Once set, remove the mousse cake from the pan, slice, and serve chilled.

Nutritional Info: Calories: 180 | Fat: 12g | Carbs: 18g | Protein: 2g

Air Fryer Function Used: None (No baking required)

Air Fryer White Chocolate Mousse Cake

Prep: 20 mins | Chill: 4 hours | Serves: 8 slices

Ingredients:
- 200g (7 oz) white chocolate, chopped
- 240ml (1 cup) heavy cream
- 2 tsp gelatin powder
- 2 tbsp cold water
- 2 tbsp hot water

Instructions:
1. In a heatproof bowl, melt the white chocolate over a saucepan of simmering water. Let it cool slightly.
2. In a small bowl, sprinkle gelatin over cold water and let it sit for 5 minutes to bloom.
3. Stir in hot water to dissolve the gelatin completely.
4. In a mixing bowl, whip the heavy cream until stiff peaks form.
5. Gently fold the melted white chocolate into the whipped cream until well combined.
6. Add the dissolved gelatin mixture to the white chocolate mousse mixture and fold gently until smooth.
7. Pour the white chocolate mousse mixture into a greased and lined cake pan that fits inside the Air Fryer basket.
8. Chill the mousse cake in the refrigerator for at least 4 hours or until set.
9. Once set, remove the mousse cake from the pan, slice, and serve chilled.

Nutritional Info: Calories: 280 | Fat: 20g | Carbs: 22g | Protein: 3g

Air Fryer Function Used: None (No baking required)

Air Fryer Bailey's Cheesecake

Prep: 20 mins | Cook: 40 mins | Chill: 4 hours | Serves: 8 slices

Ingredients:

- 200g (7 oz) digestive biscuits (graham crackers), crushed
- 75g (⅓ cup) unsalted butter, melted
- 450g (16 oz) cream cheese, softened
- 150g (¾ cup) granulated sugar
- 3 large eggs
- 120ml (½ cup) Bailey's Irish Cream liqueur
- 1 tsp vanilla extract
- Whipped cream and chocolate shavings, for garnish (optional)

Instructions:

1. Preheat your Air Fryer to 160°C (320°F).
2. In a bowl, mix the crushed digestive biscuits and melted butter until well combined.
3. Press the biscuit mixture firmly into the bottom of a greased and lined cake pan that fits inside the Air Fryer basket to form the cheesecake base.
4. In another bowl, beat the cream cheese and sugar until smooth and creamy.
5. Add the eggs, one at a time, beating well after each addition.
6. Stir in the Bailey's Irish Cream liqueur and vanilla extract until incorporated.
7. Pour the cream cheese mixture over the biscuit base in the cake pan.
8. Place the cake pan in the Air Fryer basket and cook at 160°C (320°F) for 40 minutes or until the cheesecake is set around the edges but slightly wobbly in the center.
9. Once cooked, remove the cheesecake from the Air Fryer and let it cool completely.
10. Chill the cheesecake in the refrigerator for at least 4 hours or overnight until fully set.
11. Before serving, garnish with whipped cream and chocolate shavings if desired.

Nutritional Info: Calories: 420 | Fat: 28g | Carbs: 34g | Protein: 7g

Air Fryer Function Used: Baking at 160°C (320°F)

Air Fryer Caramel Pecan Cheesecake

Prep: 20 mins | Cook: 40 mins | Chill: 4 hours | Serves: 8 slices

Ingredients:
- 200g (7 oz) digestive biscuits (graham crackers), crushed
- 75g (⅓ cup) unsalted butter, melted
- 450g (16 oz) cream cheese, softened
- 150g (¾ cup) granulated sugar
- 3 large eggs
- 120ml (½ cup) caramel sauce
- 1 tsp vanilla extract
- 100g (1 cup) pecans, chopped
- Whipped cream and extra caramel sauce, for garnish (optional)

Instructions:
1. Preheat your Air Fryer to 160°C (320°F).
2. In a bowl, mix the crushed digestive biscuits and melted butter until well combined.
3. Press the biscuit mixture firmly into the bottom of a greased and lined cake pan that fits inside the Air Fryer basket to form the cheesecake base.
4. In another bowl, beat the cream cheese and sugar until smooth and creamy.
5. Add the eggs, one at a time, beating well after each addition.
6. Stir in the caramel sauce and vanilla extract until incorporated.
7. Pour the cream cheese mixture over the biscuit base in the cake pan.
8. Sprinkle chopped pecans evenly over the top of the cheesecake mixture.
9. Place the cake pan in the Air Fryer basket and cook at 160°C (320°F) for 40 minutes or until the cheesecake is set around the edges but slightly wobbly in the center.
10. Once cooked, remove the cheesecake from the Air Fryer and let it cool completely.
11. Chill the cheesecake in the refrigerator for at least 4 hours or overnight until fully set.
12. Before serving, garnish with whipped cream and drizzle with extra caramel sauce if desired.

Nutritional Info: Calories: 450 | Fat: 32g | Carbs: 36g | Protein: 8g

Air Fryer Function Used: Baking at 160°C (320°F)

Air Fryer Key Lime Cheesecake

Prep: 20 mins | Cook: 40 mins | Chill: 4 hours | Serves: 8 slices

Ingredients:

- 200g (7 oz) digestive biscuits (graham crackers), crushed
- 75g (⅓ cup) unsalted butter, melted
- 450g (16 oz) cream cheese, softened
- 150g (¾ cup) granulated sugar
- 3 large eggs
- Zest of 3 limes
- 120ml (½ cup) fresh lime juice
- 1 tsp vanilla extract
- Lime slices and whipped cream, for garnish (optional)

Instructions:

1. Preheat your Air Fryer to 160°C (320°F).
2. In a bowl, mix the crushed digestive biscuits and melted butter until well combined.
3. Press the biscuit mixture firmly into the bottom of a greased and lined cake pan that fits inside the Air Fryer basket to form the cheesecake base.
4. In another bowl, beat the cream cheese and sugar until smooth and creamy.
5. Add the eggs, one at a time, beating well after each addition.
6. Stir in the lime zest, lime juice, and vanilla extract until incorporated.
7. Pour the cream cheese mixture over the biscuit base in the cake pan.
8. Place the cake pan in the Air Fryer basket and cook at 160°C (320°F) for 40 minutes or until the cheesecake is set around the edges but slightly wobbly in the center.
9. Once cooked, remove the cheesecake from the Air Fryer and let it cool completely.
10. Chill the cheesecake in the refrigerator for at least 4 hours or overnight until fully set.
11. Before serving, garnish with lime slices and whipped cream if desired.

Nutritional Info: Calories: 380 | Fat: 26g | Carbs: 30g | Protein: 7g

Air Fryer Function Used: Baking at 160°C (320°F)

Air Fryer Black Forest Mousse Cake

Prep: 20 mins | Chill: 4 hours | Serves: 8 slices

Ingredients:
- 200g (7 oz) dark chocolate, chopped
- 240ml (1 cup) heavy cream
- 2 tsp gelatin powder
- 2 tbsp cold water
- 2 tbsp hot water
- 200g (¾ cup) cherry pie filling
- Whipped cream and chocolate shavings, for garnish (optional)

Instructions:
1. In a heatproof bowl, melt the dark chocolate over a saucepan of simmering water. Let it cool slightly.
2. In a small bowl, sprinkle gelatin over cold water and let it sit for 5 minutes to bloom.
3. Stir in hot water to dissolve the gelatin completely.
4. In a mixing bowl, whip the heavy cream until stiff peaks form.
5. Gently fold the melted chocolate into the whipped cream until well combined.
6. Add the dissolved gelatin mixture to the chocolate mousse mixture and fold gently until smooth.
7. Pour half of the chocolate mousse mixture into a greased and lined cake pan that fits inside the Air Fryer basket.
8. Spread the cherry pie filling over the mousse layer.
9. Pour the remaining chocolate mousse mixture over the cherry filling.
10. Chill the mousse cake in the refrigerator for at least 4 hours or until set.
11. Once set, remove the mousse cake from the pan, slice, and serve chilled.

Nutritional Info: Calories: 260 | Fat: 18g | Carbs: 22g | Protein: 3g

Air Fryer Function Used: None (No baking required)

CHAPTER EIGHT: CELEBRATION AND OCCASION CAKES

Air Fryer Birthday Cake

Prep: 20 mins | Cook: 40 mins | Serves: 8-10

Ingredients:
- 200g (1 ¾ cups) all-purpose flour
- 1 ½ tsp baking powder
- ¼ tsp salt
- 100g (½ cup) unsalted butter, softened
- 150g (¾ cup) granulated sugar
- 2 large eggs
- 1 tsp vanilla extract
- 120ml (½ cup) milk
- Food coloring (optional)
- Buttercream frosting
- Sprinkles, for decoration

Instructions:
1. Preheat your Air Fryer to 160°C (320°F).
2. In a bowl, sift together the flour, baking powder, and salt.
3. In a separate bowl, cream together the softened butter and sugar until light and fluffy.
4. Beat in the eggs, one at a time, then stir in the vanilla extract.
5. Gradually mix in the dry ingredients alternating with the milk until well combined.
6. If using, divide the batter into separate bowls and add food coloring to each for a multi-colored cake.
7. Pour the batter into greased and lined cake pans that fit inside the Air Fryer basket.
8. Place the cake pans in the Air Fryer basket and bake at 160°C (320°F) for 40 minutes or until a toothpick inserted into the center comes out clean.
9. Let the cakes cool completely before removing from the pans and frosting with buttercream.
10. Decorate with sprinkles and candles before serving.

Nutritional Info: Calories: 280 | Fat: 12g | Carbs: 38g | Protein: 4g

Air Fryer Function Used: Baking at 160°C (320°F)

Air Fryer Anniversary Cake

Prep: 15 mins | Cook: 45 mins | Serves: 8-10

Ingredients:

- 250g (2 cups) self-raising flour
- ½ tsp baking powder
- 200g (1 cup) unsalted butter, softened
- 200g (1 cup) caster sugar
- 4 large eggs
- 1 tsp vanilla extract
- 2 tbsp milk
- Jam and whipped cream, for filling
- Icing sugar, for dusting

Instructions:

1. Preheat your Air Fryer to 160°C (320°F).
2. In a bowl, sift together the self-raising flour and baking powder.
3. In a separate bowl, cream together the softened butter and caster sugar until pale and fluffy.
4. Beat in the eggs, one at a time, then stir in the vanilla extract.
5. Gradually fold in the sifted flour mixture, alternating with the milk, until smooth.
6. Divide the batter evenly between two greased and lined cake pans that fit inside the Air Fryer basket.
7. Place the cake pans in the Air Fryer basket and bake at 160°C (320°F) for 45 minutes or until golden and a skewer inserted into the center comes out clean.
8. Let the cakes cool in the pans for 10 minutes before transferring to a wire rack to cool completely.
9. Once cooled, spread jam on one cake layer and top with whipped cream before placing the other cake layer on top.
10. Dust the top of the cake with icing sugar before serving.

Nutritional Info: Calories: 320 | Fat: 16g | Carbs: 40g | Protein: 5g

Air Fryer Function Used: Baking at 160°C (320°F)

Air Fryer Graduation Cake

Prep: 30 mins | Cook: 40 mins | Serves: 12

Ingredients:

- 300g (2 ½ cups) cake flour
- 2 tsp baking powder
- ½ tsp salt
- 150g (¾ cup) unsalted butter, softened
- 200g (1 cup) granulated sugar
- 4 large eggs
- 1 tsp vanilla extract
- 180ml (¾ cup) milk
- 2 tbsp cocoa powder
- Buttercream frosting
- Fondant (optional)
- Edible decorations (optional)

Instructions:

1. Preheat your Air Fryer to 160°C (320°F).
2. In a bowl, sift together the cake flour, baking powder, and salt.
3. In another bowl, cream together the softened butter and granulated sugar until light and fluffy.
4. Beat in the eggs, one at a time, then stir in the vanilla extract.
5. Gradually mix in the dry ingredients alternating with the milk until well combined.
6. Divide the batter evenly into two bowls.
7. Mix cocoa powder into one bowl of batter to create chocolate batter.
8. Pour the vanilla and chocolate batters into greased and lined cake pans that fit inside the Air Fryer basket.
9. Use a toothpick to swirl the batters together for a marble effect.
10. Place the cake pans in the Air Fryer basket and bake at 160°C (320°F) for 40 minutes or until a toothpick inserted into the center comes out clean.
11. Let the cakes cool completely before frosting with buttercream.
12. Decorate with fondant and edible decorations if desired.

Nutritional Info: Calories: 280 | Fat: 14g | Carbs: 34g | Protein: 4g

Air Fryer Function Used: Baking at 160°C (320°F)

Air Fryer Wedding Cake

Prep: 45 mins | Cook: 1 hour | Serves: 20-30 (depending on tiers)

Ingredients:

- For each tier: (multiply ingredients as needed)
- 400g (3 ¼ cups) cake flour
- 2 tsp baking powder
- ½ tsp salt
- 225g (1 cup) unsalted butter, softened
- 300g (1 ½ cups) granulated sugar
- 5 large eggs
- 2 tsp vanilla extract
- 240ml (1 cup) milk
- Buttercream frosting
- Fondant
- Edible flowers or decorations

Instructions:

1. Preheat your Air Fryer to 160°C (320°F).
2. For each tier, follow the same steps: In a bowl, sift together the cake flour, baking powder, and salt.
3. In another bowl, cream together the softened butter and granulated sugar until light and fluffy.
4. Beat in the eggs, one at a time, then stir in the vanilla extract.
5. Gradually mix in the dry ingredients alternating with the milk until well combined.
6. Pour the batter into greased and lined cake pans of various sizes to create tiers that fit inside the Air Fryer basket.
7. Place the cake pans in the Air Fryer basket and bake at 160°C (320°F) for 1 hour or until a toothpick inserted into the center comes out clean.
8. Let the cakes cool completely before stacking and frosting with buttercream.
9. Roll out fondant and cover each tier, smoothing it over the surface.
10. Decorate with edible flowers or other decorations as desired.

Nutritional Info: Calories: Varies | Fat: Varies | Carbs: Varies | Protein: Varies

Air Fryer Function Used: Baking at 160°C (320°F)

Air Fryer Gingerbread House

Prep: 45 mins | Cook: 30 mins | Serves: 1 gingerbread house

Ingredients:

- 350g (2 ¾ cups) all-purpose flour
- 1 tsp baking soda
- 1 ½ tsp ground ginger
- 1 tsp ground cinnamon
- ¼ tsp ground cloves
- ¼ tsp salt
- 115g (½ cup) unsalted butter, softened
- 100g (½ cup) dark brown sugar
- 1 large egg
- 120ml (½ cup) molasses
- Royal icing (for assembling)
- Assorted candies and decorations

Instructions:

1. Preheat your Air Fryer to 160°C (320°F).
2. In a bowl, sift together the flour, baking soda, ground ginger, ground cinnamon, ground cloves, and salt.
3. In another bowl, cream together the softened butter and dark brown sugar until light and fluffy.
4. Beat in the egg, then stir in the molasses until well combined.
5. Gradually mix in the dry ingredients until a dough forms.
6. Divide the dough into smaller portions and roll out on a floured surface to about ¼ inch thickness.
7. Use gingerbread house templates or cutters to cut out the shapes for the house walls, roof, and other pieces.
8. Place the gingerbread pieces on a parchment-lined baking sheet and bake in the Air Fryer at 160°C (320°F) for 10-12 minutes or until firm and lightly browned.
9. Let the gingerbread pieces cool completely before assembling the house using royal icing as glue.
10. Decorate the gingerbread house with assorted candies and decorations as desired.

Nutritional Info: Calories: 250 | Fat: 7g | Carbs: 45g | Protein: 3g

Air Fryer Function Used: Baking at 160°C (320°F)

Air Fryer Christmas Cake

Prep: 30 mins | Cook: 1 hour 30 mins | Serves: 12

Ingredients:
- 300g (2 cups) mixed dried fruit (raisins, sultanas, currants)
- 150ml (⅔ cup) brandy
- 200g (1 ¾ cups) all-purpose flour
- 1 tsp baking powder
- ½ tsp ground cinnamon
- ¼ tsp ground nutmeg
- 200g (1 cup) unsalted butter, softened
- 200g (1 cup) light brown sugar
- 4 large eggs
- 1 tsp vanilla extract
- Zest of 1 orange
- Zest of 1 lemon
- 50g (⅓ cup) chopped almonds
- Marzipan and icing for decoration

Instructions:
1. In a bowl, combine the mixed dried fruit with the brandy and let it soak overnight.
2. Preheat your Air Fryer to 150°C (300°F).
3. In a separate bowl, sift together the flour, baking powder, cinnamon, and nutmeg.
4. In another bowl, cream together the softened butter and light brown sugar until light and fluffy.
5. Beat in the eggs, one at a time, then stir in the vanilla extract.
6. Gradually mix in the dry ingredients until well combined.
7. Fold in the soaked dried fruit mixture, chopped almonds, orange zest, and lemon zest.
8. Pour the batter into a greased and lined cake pan that fits inside the Air Fryer basket.
9. Place the cake pan in the Air Fryer basket and bake at 150°C (300°F) for 1 hour 30 minutes or until a skewer inserted into the center comes out clean.
10. Let the cake cool completely before decorating with marzipan and icing.

Nutritional Info: Calories: 320 | Fat: 14g | Carbs: 45g | Protein: 5g

Air Fryer Function Used: Baking at 150°C (300°F)

Air Fryer Easter Cake

Prep: 20 mins | Cook: 40 mins | Serves: 8-10

Ingredients:
- 200g (1 ¾ cups) all-purpose flour
- 1 ½ tsp baking powder
- ¼ tsp salt
- 100g (½ cup) unsalted butter, softened
- 150g (¾ cup) granulated sugar
- 2 large eggs
- 1 tsp vanilla extract
- 120ml (½ cup) milk
- Zest of 1 lemon
- Zest of 1 orange
- 100g (¾ cup) mixed dried fruit (raisins, sultanas, currants)
- Icing sugar, for dusting

Instructions:
1. Preheat your Air Fryer to 160°C (320°F).
2. In a bowl, sift together the flour, baking powder, and salt.
3. In another bowl, cream together the softened butter and granulated sugar until light and fluffy.
4. Beat in the eggs, one at a time, then stir in the vanilla extract.
5. Gradually mix in the dry ingredients alternating with the milk until well combined.
6. Fold in the lemon zest, orange zest, and mixed dried fruit until evenly distributed.
7. Pour the batter into a greased and lined cake pan that fits inside the Air Fryer basket.
8. Place the cake pan in the Air Fryer basket and bake at 160°C (320°F) for 40 minutes or until a toothpick inserted into the center comes out clean.
9. Let the cake cool in the pan for 10 minutes before transferring to a wire rack to cool completely.
10. Dust the top of the cake with icing sugar before serving.

Nutritional Info: Calories: 240 | Fat: 9g | Carbs: 36g | Protein: 4g

Air Fryer Function Used: Baking at 160°C (320°F)

Air Fryer Mother's Day Cake

Prep: 25 mins | Cook: 45 mins | Serves: 8-10

Ingredients:

- 250g (2 cups) self-raising flour
- ½ tsp baking powder
- 200g (1 cup) unsalted butter, softened
- 200g (1 cup) caster sugar
- 4 large eggs
- 1 tsp vanilla extract
- 2 tbsp milk
- Buttercream frosting
- Fresh flowers or edible decorations

Instructions:

1. Preheat your Air Fryer to 160°C (320°F).
2. In a bowl, sift together the self-raising flour and baking powder.
3. In another bowl, cream together the softened butter and caster sugar until pale and fluffy.
4. Beat in the eggs, one at a time, then stir in the vanilla extract.
5. Gradually fold in the sifted flour mixture, alternating with the milk, until smooth.
6. Pour the batter into a greased and lined cake pan that fits inside the Air Fryer basket.
7. Place the cake pan in the Air Fryer basket and bake at 160°C (320°F) for 45 minutes or until golden and a skewer inserted into the center comes out clean.
8. Let the cake cool in the pan for 10 minutes before transferring to a wire rack to cool completely.
9. Once cooled, frost the cake with buttercream and decorate with fresh flowers or edible decorations before serving.

Nutritional Info: Calories: 280 | Fat: 14g | Carbs: 36g | Protein: 4g

Air Fryer Function Used: Baking at 160°C (320°F)

Air Fryer Father's Day Cake

Prep: 20 mins | Cook: 35 mins | Serves: 8-10

Ingredients:

- 200g (1 ¾ cups) all-purpose flour
- 1 ½ tsp baking powder
- ¼ tsp salt
- 100g (½ cup) unsalted butter, softened
- 150g (¾ cup) granulated sugar
- 2 large eggs
- 1 tsp vanilla extract
- 120ml (½ cup) milk
- 50g (⅓ cup) chopped nuts (such as walnuts or pecans)
- 50g (⅓ cup) chocolate chips (optional)
- Whipped cream or frosting for serving

Instructions:

1. Preheat your Air Fryer to 160°C (320°F).
2. In a bowl, sift together the flour, baking powder, and salt.
3. In another bowl, cream together the softened butter and granulated sugar until light and fluffy.
4. Beat in the eggs, one at a time, then stir in the vanilla extract.
5. Gradually mix in the dry ingredients alternating with the milk until well combined.
6. Fold in the chopped nuts and chocolate chips, if using.
7. Pour the batter into a greased and lined cake pan that fits inside the Air Fryer basket.
8. Place the cake pan in the Air Fryer basket and bake at 160°C (320°F) for 35 minutes or until a toothpick inserted into the center comes out clean.
9. Let the cake cool in the pan for 10 minutes before transferring to a wire rack to cool completely.
10. Serve slices of cake with whipped cream or frosting.

Nutritional Info: Calories: 240 | Fat: 10g | Carbs: 32g | Protein: 4g

Air Fryer Function Used: Baking at 160°C (320°F)

Air Fryer Halloween Cake

Prep: 30 mins | Cook: 40 mins | Serves: 8-10

Ingredients:
- 200g (1 ¾ cups) all-purpose flour
- 1 ½ tsp baking powder
- ¼ tsp salt
- 100g (½ cup) unsalted butter, softened
- 150g (¾ cup) granulated sugar
- 2 large eggs
- 1 tsp vanilla extract
- 120ml (½ cup) milk
- Orange food coloring
- Black food coloring
- Buttercream frosting
- Halloween-themed decorations

Instructions:
1. Preheat your Air Fryer to 160°C (320°F).
2. In a bowl, sift together the flour, baking powder, and salt.
3. In another bowl, cream together the softened butter and granulated sugar until light and fluffy.
4. Beat in the eggs, one at a time, then stir in the vanilla extract.
5. Gradually mix in the dry ingredients alternating with the milk until well combined.
6. Divide the batter into two bowls.
7. Add orange food coloring to one bowl and black food coloring to the other, mixing until evenly colored.
8. Pour the colored batters into greased and lined cake pans that fit inside the Air Fryer basket.
9. Place the cake pans in the Air Fryer basket and bake at 160°C (320°F) for 40 minutes or until a toothpick inserted into the center comes out clean.
10. Let the cakes cool completely before frosting with buttercream and decorating with Halloween-themed decorations.

Nutritional Info: Calories: 250 | Fat: 10g | Carbs: 35g | Protein: 4g

Air Fryer Function Used: Baking at 160°C (320°F)

Air Fryer New Year's Eve Cake

Prep: 30 mins | Cook: 40 mins | Serves: 8-10

Ingredients:
- 200g (1 ¾ cups) all-purpose flour
- 1 ½ tsp baking powder
- ¼ tsp salt
- 100g (½ cup) unsalted butter, softened
- 150g (¾ cup) granulated sugar
- 2 large eggs
- 1 tsp vanilla extract
- 120ml (½ cup) milk
- Sprinkles or edible glitter
- Whipped cream or frosting for serving

Instructions:
1. Preheat your Air Fryer to 160°C (320°F).
2. In a bowl, sift together the flour, baking powder, and salt.
3. In another bowl, cream together the softened butter and granulated sugar until light and fluffy.
4. Beat in the eggs, one at a time, then stir in the vanilla extract.
5. Gradually mix in the dry ingredients alternating with the milk until well combined.
6. Pour the batter into a greased and lined cake pan that fits inside the Air Fryer basket.
7. Place the cake pan in the Air Fryer basket and bake at 160°C (320°F) for 40 minutes or until a toothpick inserted into the center comes out clean.
8. Let the cake cool in the pan for 10 minutes before transferring to a wire rack to cool completely.
9. Once cooled, frost the cake with whipped cream or frosting and decorate with sprinkles or edible glitter.
10. Serve slices of cake for your New Year's Eve celebration!

Nutritional Info: Calories: 240 | Fat: 10g | Carbs: 32g | Protein: 4g

Air Fryer Function Used: Baking at 160°C (320°F)

Air Fryer Valentine's Day Cake

Prep: 25 mins | Cook: 35 mins | Serves: 8-10

Ingredients:
- 200g (1 ¾ cups) all-purpose flour
- 1 ½ tsp baking powder
- ¼ tsp salt
- 100g (½ cup) unsalted butter, softened
- 150g (¾ cup) granulated sugar
- 2 large eggs
- 1 tsp vanilla extract
- 120ml (½ cup) milk
- Red food coloring
- Whipped cream or frosting for serving

Instructions:
1. Preheat your Air Fryer to 160°C (320°F).
2. In a bowl, sift together the flour, baking powder, and salt.
3. In another bowl, cream together the softened butter and granulated sugar until light and fluffy.
4. Beat in the eggs, one at a time, then stir in the vanilla extract.
5. Gradually mix in the dry ingredients alternating with the milk until well combined.
6. Add red food coloring to the batter, mixing until evenly colored.
7. Pour the batter into a greased and lined cake pan that fits inside the Air Fryer basket.
8. Place the cake pan in the Air Fryer basket and bake at 160°C (320°F) for 35 minutes or until a toothpick inserted into the center comes out clean.
9. Let the cake cool in the pan for 10 minutes before transferring to a wire rack to cool completely.
10. Once cooled, frost the cake with whipped cream or frosting and serve as a delightful treat for Valentine's Day!

Nutritional Info: Calories: 240 | Fat: 10g | Carbs: 32g | Protein: 4g

Air Fryer Function Used: Baking at 160°C (320°F)

Air Fryer St. Patrick's Day Cake

Prep: 25 mins | Cook: 35 mins | Serves: 8-10

Ingredients:

- 200g (1 ¾ cups) all-purpose flour
- 1 ½ tsp baking powder
- ¼ tsp salt
- 100g (½ cup) unsalted butter, softened
- 150g (¾ cup) granulated sugar
- 2 large eggs
- 1 tsp vanilla extract
- 120ml (½ cup) milk
- Green food coloring
- Whipped cream or frosting for serving
- Shamrock-shaped sprinkles or decorations

Instructions:

1. Preheat your Air Fryer to 160°C (320°F).
2. In a bowl, sift together the flour, baking powder, and salt.
3. In another bowl, cream together the softened butter and granulated sugar until light and fluffy.
4. Beat in the eggs, one at a time, then stir in the vanilla extract.
5. Gradually mix in the dry ingredients alternating with the milk until well combined.
6. Add green food coloring to the batter, mixing until evenly colored.
7. Pour the batter into a greased and lined cake pan that fits inside the Air Fryer basket.
8. Place the cake pan in the Air Fryer basket and bake at 160°C (320°F) for 35 minutes or until a toothpick inserted into the center comes out clean.
9. Let the cake cool in the pan for 10 minutes before transferring to a wire rack to cool completely.
10. Once cooled, frost the cake with whipped cream or frosting and decorate with shamrock-shaped sprinkles or decorations for a festive St. Patrick's Day treat!

Nutritional Info: Calories: 240 | Fat: 10g | Carbs: 32g | Protein: 4g

Air Fryer Function Used: Baking at 160°C (320°F)

Air Fryer Thanksgiving Cake

Prep: 30 mins | Cook: 40 mins | Serves: 8-10

Ingredients:
- 200g (1 ¾ cups) all-purpose flour
- 1 ½ tsp baking powder
- ¼ tsp salt
- 100g (½ cup) unsalted butter, softened
- 150g (¾ cup) granulated sugar
- 2 large eggs
- 1 tsp vanilla extract
- 120ml (½ cup) milk
- 150g (1 cup) canned pumpkin puree
- 1 tsp ground cinnamon
- ½ tsp ground nutmeg
- ¼ tsp ground cloves
- Whipped cream or frosting for serving
- Pecan halves or caramel sauce for topping

Instructions:
1. Preheat your Air Fryer to 160°C (320°F).
2. In a bowl, sift together the flour, baking powder, and salt.
3. In another bowl, cream together the softened butter and granulated sugar until light and fluffy.
4. Beat in the eggs, one at a time, then stir in the vanilla extract.
5. Gradually mix in the dry ingredients alternating with the milk until well combined.
6. Stir in the canned pumpkin puree, ground cinnamon, ground nutmeg, and ground cloves until evenly incorporated.
7. Pour the batter into a greased and lined cake pan that fits inside the Air Fryer basket.
8. Place the cake pan in the Air Fryer basket and bake at 160°C (320°F) for 40 minutes or until a toothpick inserted into the center comes out clean.
9. Let the cake cool in the pan for 10 minutes before transferring to a wire rack to cool completely.
10. Once cooled, frost the cake with whipped cream or frosting and top with pecan halves or drizzle with caramel sauce for a Thanksgiving-inspired dessert!

Nutritional Info: Calories: 250 | Fat: 10g | Carbs: 35g | Protein: 4g

Air Fryer Function Used: Baking at 160°C (320°F)

Air Fryer Cinco de Mayo Cake

Prep: 25 mins | Cook: 35 mins | Serves: 8-10

Ingredients:
- 200g (1 ¾ cups) all-purpose flour
- 1 ½ tsp baking powder
- ¼ tsp salt
- 100g (½ cup) unsalted butter, softened
- 150g (¾ cup) granulated sugar
- 2 large eggs
- 1 tsp vanilla extract
- 120ml (½ cup) milk
- Zest of 1 lime
- 2 tbsp tequila (optional)
- 1 tbsp triple sec (optional)
- Whipped cream or frosting for serving
- Lime slices for garnish

Instructions:
1. Preheat your Air Fryer to 160°C (320°F).
2. In a bowl, sift together the flour, baking powder, and salt.
3. In another bowl, cream together the softened butter and granulated sugar until light and fluffy.
4. Beat in the eggs, one at a time, then stir in the vanilla extract.
5. Gradually mix in the dry ingredients alternating with the milk until well combined.
6. Stir in the lime zest, tequila (if using), and triple sec (if using) until evenly incorporated.
7. Pour the batter into a greased and lined cake pan that fits inside the Air Fryer basket.
8. Place the cake pan in the Air Fryer basket and bake at 160°C (320°F) for 35 minutes or until a toothpick inserted into the center comes out clean.
9. Let the cake cool in the pan for 10 minutes before transferring to a wire rack to cool completely.
10. Once cooled, frost the cake with whipped cream or frosting and garnish with lime slices for a festive Cinco de Mayo dessert!

Nutritional Info: Calories: 250 | Fat: 10g | Carbs: 35g | Protein: 4g

Air Fryer Function Used: Baking at 160°C (320°F)

Air Fryer Bastille Day Cake

Prep: 25 mins | Cook: 35 mins | Serves: 8-10

Ingredients:
- 200g (1 ¾ cups) all-purpose flour
- 1 ½ tsp baking powder
- ¼ tsp salt
- 100g (½ cup) unsalted butter, softened
- 150g (¾ cup) granulated sugar
- 2 large eggs
- 1 tsp vanilla extract
- 120ml (½ cup) milk
- 100g (¾ cup) fresh raspberries
- 100g (¾ cup) fresh blueberries
- Whipped cream or frosting for serving

Instructions:
1. Preheat your Air Fryer to 160°C (320°F).
2. In a bowl, sift together the flour, baking powder, and salt.
3. In another bowl, cream together the softened butter and granulated sugar until light and fluffy.
4. Beat in the eggs, one at a time, then stir in the vanilla extract.
5. Gradually mix in the dry ingredients alternating with the milk until well combined.
6. Gently fold in the fresh raspberries and blueberries until evenly distributed.
7. Pour the batter into a greased and lined cake pan that fits inside the Air Fryer basket.
8. Place the cake pan in the Air Fryer basket and bake at 160°C (320°F) for 35 minutes or until a toothpick inserted into the center comes out clean.
9. Let the cake cool in the pan for 10 minutes before transferring to a wire rack to cool completely.
10. Once cooled, frost the cake with whipped cream or frosting and serve as a delicious dessert to celebrate Bastille Day!

Nutritional Info: Calories: 250 | Fat: 10g | Carbs: 35g | Protein: 4g

Air Fryer Function Used: Baking at 160°C (320°F)

CHAPTER NINE: GLUTEN-FREE AND VEGAN DELIGHTS

Air Fryer Decadent Gluten-Free Chocolate Cake

Prep: 15 mins | Cook: 40 mins | Serves: 8-10

Ingredients:
- 1 ½ cups (180g) gluten-free all-purpose flour
- 1 cup (200g) granulated sugar
- ½ cup (50g) unsweetened cocoa powder
- 1 tsp baking powder
- ½ tsp baking soda
- ½ tsp salt
- 1 cup (240ml) almond milk (or any plant-based milk)
- ⅓ cup (80ml) vegetable oil
- 1 tsp vanilla extract
- 1 tbsp apple cider vinegar
- Vegan chocolate chips (optional, for topping)

Instructions:
1. Preheat your Air Fryer to 160°C (320°F).
2. In a large mixing bowl, sift together the gluten-free flour, sugar, cocoa powder, baking powder, baking soda, and salt.
3. In a separate bowl, whisk together the almond milk, vegetable oil, vanilla extract, and apple cider vinegar.
4. Pour the wet ingredients into the dry ingredients and mix until smooth and well combined.
5. Grease and line a cake pan that fits inside the Air Fryer basket.
6. Pour the batter into the prepared cake pan and smooth out the top with a spatula.
7. Sprinkle vegan chocolate chips on top if desired.
8. Place the cake pan in the Air Fryer basket and bake at 160°C (320°F) for 40 minutes or until a toothpick inserted into the center comes out clean.
9. Once baked, remove the cake from the Air Fryer and let it cool in the pan for 10 minutes before transferring it to a wire rack to cool completely.
10. Slice and serve this indulgent gluten-free chocolate cake!

Nutritional Info: Calories: 220 | Fat: 10g | Carbs: 32g | Protein: 3g

Air Fryer Function Used: Baking at 160°C (320°F)

Air Fryer Moist Gluten-Free Carrot Cake

Prep: 20 mins | Cook: 45 mins | Serves: 8-10

Ingredients:
- 1 ½ cups (180g) gluten-free all-purpose flour
- 1 cup (200g) granulated sugar
- 1 tsp baking powder
- 1 tsp baking soda
- ½ tsp salt
- 1 tsp ground cinnamon
- ½ tsp ground nutmeg
- ½ cup (120ml) vegetable oil
- 2 flax eggs (2 tbsp ground flaxseed + 6 tbsp water)
- 1 tsp vanilla extract
- 1 ½ cups (150g) grated carrots
- ½ cup (50g) chopped walnuts or pecans (optional)
- ½ cup (75g) raisins (optional)
- Vegan cream cheese frosting (optional, for topping)

1. Instructions:
1. Preheat your Air Fryer to 160°C (320°F).
2. In a large mixing bowl, whisk together the gluten-free flour, sugar, baking powder, baking soda, salt, cinnamon, and nutmeg.
3. In another bowl, prepare the flax eggs by mixing together ground flaxseed and water. Let it sit for 5 minutes until it thickens.
4. Add the vegetable oil, prepared flax eggs, and vanilla extract to the dry ingredients. Mix until well combined.
5. Fold in the grated carrots, chopped nuts, and raisins if using.
6. Grease and line a cake pan that fits inside the Air Fryer basket.
7. Pour the batter into the prepared cake pan and smooth out the top with a spatula.
8. Place the cake pan in the Air Fryer basket and bake at 160°C (320°F) for 45 minutes or until a toothpick inserted into the center comes out clean.

9. Once baked, remove the cake from the Air Fryer and let it cool in the pan for 10 minutes before transferring it to a wire rack to cool completely.
10. Optionally, frost the cooled cake with vegan cream cheese frosting.
11. Slice and serve this moist gluten-free carrot cake!

Nutritional Info: Calories: 230 | Fat: 12g | Carbs: 30g | Protein: 3g

Air Fryer Function Used: Baking at 160°C (320°F)

Air Fryer Tangy Gluten-Free Lemon Cake

Prep: 15 mins | Cook: 35 mins | Serves: 8-10

Ingredients:
- 1 ½ cups (180g) gluten-free all-purpose flour
- 1 cup (200g) granulated sugar
- Zest of 2 lemons
- 1 tsp baking powder
- ½ tsp baking soda
- ¼ tsp salt
- ½ cup (120ml) unsweetened almond milk (or any plant-based milk)
- ⅓ cup (80ml) vegetable oil
- 2 tbsp lemon juice
- 1 tsp vanilla extract
- Lemon glaze (optional, made with powdered sugar and lemon juice)

Instructions:
1. Preheat your Air Fryer to 160°C (320°F).
2. In a large mixing bowl, whisk together the gluten-free flour, sugar, lemon zest, baking powder, baking soda, and salt.
3. In another bowl, mix together the almond milk, vegetable oil, lemon juice, and vanilla extract.
4. Pour the wet ingredients into the dry ingredients and mix until well combined.
5. Grease and line a cake pan that fits inside the Air Fryer basket.
6. Pour the batter into the prepared cake pan and smooth out the top with a spatula.

7. Place the cake pan in the Air Fryer basket and bake at 160°C (320°F) for 35 minutes or until a toothpick inserted into the center comes out clean.
8. Once baked, remove the cake from the Air Fryer and let it cool in the pan for 10 minutes before transferring it to a wire rack to cool completely.
9. If desired, drizzle the cooled cake with lemon glaze for an extra tangy flavor.
10. Slice and serve this delightful gluten-free lemon cake!

Nutritional Info: Calories: 220 | Fat: 10g | Carbs: 30g | Protein: 2g

Air Fryer Function Used: Baking at 160°C (320°F)

Air Fryer Rich Vegan Chocolate Cake

Prep: 20 mins | Cook: 40 mins | Serves: 8-10

Ingredients:
- 1 ½ cups (180g) all-purpose flour (check for gluten-free if needed)
- 1 cup (200g) granulated sugar
- ½ cup (50g) unsweetened cocoa powder
- 1 tsp baking powder
- ½ tsp baking soda
- ½ tsp salt
- 1 cup (240ml) almond milk (or any plant-based milk)
- ⅓ cup (80ml) vegetable oil
- 2 tsp vanilla extract
- 1 tbsp apple cider vinegar
- Vegan chocolate chips (optional, for topping)

Instructions:

1. Preheat your Air Fryer to 160°C (320°F).
2. In a large mixing bowl, sift together the all-purpose flour, sugar, cocoa powder, baking powder, baking soda, and salt.
3. In another bowl, whisk together the almond milk, vegetable oil, vanilla extract, and apple cider vinegar.
4. Pour the wet ingredients into the dry ingredients and mix until smooth and well combined.
5. Grease and line a cake pan that fits inside the Air Fryer basket.
6. Pour the batter into the prepared cake pan and smooth out the top with a spatula.
7. Sprinkle vegan chocolate chips on top if desired.
8. Place the cake pan in the Air Fryer basket and bake at 160°C (320°F) for 40 minutes or until a toothpick inserted into the center comes out clean.
9. Once baked, remove the cake from the Air Fryer and let it cool in the pan for 10 minutes before transferring it to a wire rack to cool completely.
10. Slice and serve this rich vegan chocolate cake for a decadent treat!

Nutritional Info: Calories: 240 | Fat: 12g | Carbs: 32g | Protein: 3g

Air Fryer Function Used: Baking at 160°C (320°F)

Air Fryer Moist Vegan Banana Bread

Prep: 15 mins | Cook: 45 mins | Serves: 8-10

Ingredients:

- 1 ¾ cups (210g) all-purpose flour (check for gluten-free if needed)
- 1 tsp baking soda
- ½ tsp baking powder
- ½ tsp salt
- ⅓ cup (80ml) vegetable oil
- ⅔ cup (130g) granulated sugar
- 4 ripe bananas, mashed
- ¼ cup (60ml) almond milk (or any plant-based milk)
- 1 tsp vanilla extract
- Vegan chocolate chips or chopped nuts (optional, for topping)

Instructions:

1. Preheat your Air Fryer to 160°C (320°F).
2. In a large mixing bowl, sift together the all-purpose flour, baking soda, baking powder, and salt.
3. In another bowl, whisk together the vegetable oil and granulated sugar until well combined.
4. Add the mashed bananas, almond milk, and vanilla extract to the oil-sugar mixture. Mix until smooth.
5. Gradually add the dry ingredients to the wet ingredients, stirring until just combined. Do not overmix.
6. Grease and line a loaf pan that fits inside the Air Fryer basket.
7. Pour the batter into the prepared loaf pan and smooth out the top with a spatula.
8. Sprinkle vegan chocolate chips or chopped nuts on top if desired.
9. Place the loaf pan in the Air Fryer basket and bake at 160°C (320°F) for 45 minutes or until a toothpick inserted into the center comes out clean.
10. Once baked, remove the banana bread from the Air Fryer and let it cool in the pan for 10 minutes before transferring it to a wire rack to cool completely.
11. Slice and enjoy this moist vegan banana bread as a delicious snack or breakfast treat!

Nutritional Info: Calories: 200 | Fat: 8g | Carbs: 30g | Protein: 2g

Air Fryer Function Used: Baking at 160°C (320°F)

Air Fryer Vegan Pumpkin Bread

Prep: 20 mins | Cook: 40 mins | Serves: 8-10

Ingredients:

- 1 ¾ cups (210g) all-purpose flour (check for gluten-free if needed)
- 1 tsp baking soda
- ½ tsp baking powder
- ½ tsp salt
- 1 tsp ground cinnamon
- ½ tsp ground nutmeg
- ¼ tsp ground cloves
- ⅓ cup (80ml) vegetable oil
- ⅔ cup (130g) granulated sugar

- 1 cup (240g) pumpkin puree
- ¼ cup (60ml) almond milk (or any plant-based milk)
- 1 tsp vanilla extract
- Vegan chocolate chips or chopped nuts (optional, for topping)

Instructions:

1. Preheat your Air Fryer to 160°C (320°F).
2. In a large mixing bowl, sift together the all-purpose flour, baking soda, baking powder, salt, cinnamon, nutmeg, and cloves.
3. In another bowl, whisk together the vegetable oil and granulated sugar until well combined.
4. Add the pumpkin puree, almond milk, and vanilla extract to the oil-sugar mixture. Mix until smooth.
5. Gradually add the dry ingredients to the wet ingredients, stirring until just combined. Do not overmix.
6. Grease and line a loaf pan that fits inside the Air Fryer basket.
7. Pour the batter into the prepared loaf pan and smooth out the top with a spatula.
8. Sprinkle vegan chocolate chips or chopped nuts on top if desired.
9. Place the loaf pan in the Air Fryer basket and bake at 160°C (320°F) for 40 minutes or until a toothpick inserted into the center comes out clean.
10. Once baked, remove the pumpkin bread from the Air Fryer and let it cool in the pan for 10 minutes before transferring it to a wire rack to cool completely.
11. Slice and enjoy this deliciously moist vegan pumpkin bread!

Nutritional Info: Calories: 220 | Fat: 9g | Carbs: 32g | Protein: 2g

Air Fryer Function Used: Baking at 160°C (320°F)

Air Fryer Vegan Zucchini Bread

Prep: 15 mins | Cook: 45 mins | Serves: 8-10

Ingredients:
- 1 ¾ cups (210g) all-purpose flour (check for gluten-free if needed)
- 1 tsp baking soda
- ½ tsp baking powder
- ½ tsp salt
- 1 tsp ground cinnamon
- ¼ tsp ground nutmeg
- ⅓ cup (80ml) vegetable oil
- ⅔ cup (130g) granulated sugar
- 1 cup (200g) shredded zucchini
- ¼ cup (60ml) almond milk (or any plant-based milk)
- 1 tsp vanilla extract
- Vegan chocolate chips or chopped nuts (optional, for topping)

Instructions:
1. Preheat your Air Fryer to 160°C (320°F).
2. In a large mixing bowl, sift together the all-purpose flour, baking soda, baking powder, salt, cinnamon, and nutmeg.
3. In another bowl, whisk together the vegetable oil and granulated sugar until well combined.
4. Add the shredded zucchini, almond milk, and vanilla extract to the oil-sugar mixture. Mix until smooth.
5. Gradually add the dry ingredients to the wet ingredients, stirring until just combined. Do not overmix.
6. Grease and line a loaf pan that fits inside the Air Fryer basket.
7. Pour the batter into the prepared loaf pan and smooth out the top with a spatula.
8. Sprinkle vegan chocolate chips or chopped nuts on top if desired.
9. Place the loaf pan in the Air Fryer basket and bake at 160°C (320°F) for 45 minutes or until a toothpick inserted into the center comes out clean.
10. Once baked, remove the zucchini bread from the Air Fryer and let it cool in the pan for 10 minutes before transferring it to a wire rack to cool completely.
11. Slice and enjoy this moist and flavorful vegan zucchini bread!

Nutritional Info: Calories: 210 | Fat: 8g | Carbs: 30g | Protein: 2g

Air Fryer Function Used: Baking at 160°C (320°F)

Air Fryer Gluten-Free Muffins

Prep: 15 mins | Cook: 20 mins | Serves: 8-10

Ingredients:

- 1 ½ cups (180g) gluten-free all-purpose flour
- ½ cup (100g) granulated sugar
- 2 tsp baking powder
- ½ tsp baking soda
- ¼ tsp salt
- ½ cup (120ml) almond milk (or any plant-based milk)
- ⅓ cup (80ml) vegetable oil
- 1 tsp vanilla extract
- 1 flax egg (1 tbsp ground flaxseed + 3 tbsp water)
- 1 cup (150g) fresh blueberries or other fruits
- Vegan butter or jam for serving (optional)

Instructions:

1. Preheat your Air Fryer to 180°C (350°F).
2. In a large mixing bowl, sift together the gluten-free flour, sugar, baking powder, baking soda, and salt.
3. In another bowl, prepare the flax egg by mixing together ground flaxseed and water. Let it sit for 5 minutes to thicken.
4. Add the almond milk, vegetable oil, vanilla extract, and prepared flax egg to the dry ingredients. Mix until well combined.
5. Gently fold in the fresh blueberries or other fruits until evenly distributed.
6. Line muffin cups with paper liners or lightly grease them.
7. Spoon the muffin batter into the prepared muffin cups, filling each about two-thirds full.
8. Place the muffin tin in the Air Fryer basket, ensuring there is space between each muffin.
9. Air fry at 180°C (350°F) for about 18-20 minutes or until the muffins are golden brown and a toothpick inserted into the center comes out clean.
10. Once baked, remove the muffins from the Air Fryer and let them cool in the muffin tin for a few minutes.
11. Transfer the muffins to a wire rack to cool completely before serving.
12. Serve the gluten-free muffins with vegan butter or jam if desired.
13. Enjoy these delightful gluten-free muffins as a tasty breakfast or snack option!

Nutritional Info: Calories: 180 | Fat: 8g | Carbs: 26g | Protein: 2g

Air Fryer Function Used: Baking at 180°C (350°F)

Air Fryer Vegan Cupcakes

Prep: 15 mins | Cook: 18 mins | Makes: 12 cupcakes

Ingredients:

- 1 ½ cups (180g) all-purpose flour
- 1 cup (200g) granulated sugar
- 1 tsp baking powder
- ½ tsp baking soda
- ¼ tsp salt
- 1 cup (240ml) almond milk (or any plant-based milk)
- ⅓ cup (80ml) vegetable oil
- 1 tbsp apple cider vinegar
- 1 tsp vanilla extract
- Vegan frosting of your choice (optional)

Instructions:

1. Preheat the Air Fryer to 180°C (350°F).
2. In a large mixing bowl, sift together the all-purpose flour, sugar, baking powder, baking soda, and salt.
3. In another bowl, mix together the almond milk, vegetable oil, apple cider vinegar, and vanilla extract.
4. Pour the wet ingredients into the dry ingredients and stir until just combined. Be careful not to overmix.
5. Line a muffin tin with cupcake liners.
6. Spoon the batter evenly into the cupcake liners, filling each about two-thirds full.
7. Place the muffin tin in the Air Fryer basket, leaving space between each cupcake.
8. Air fry at 180°C (350°F) for 18 minutes or until a toothpick inserted into the center of a cupcake comes out clean.
9. Once baked, remove the cupcakes from the Air Fryer and let them cool completely on a wire rack.
10. Once cooled, frost the cupcakes with your favorite vegan frosting, if desired.
11. Serve and enjoy these fluffy and delicious vegan cupcakes!

Nutritional Info: Calories: 180 | Fat: 8g | Carbs: 26g | Protein: 2g

Air Fryer Function Used: Baking at 180°C (350°F)

Air Fryer Vegan Brownies

Prep: 15 mins | Cook: 25 mins | Makes: 9 brownies

Ingredients:
- ¾ cup (90g) all-purpose flour
- ½ cup (50g) unsweetened cocoa powder
- ½ tsp baking powder
- ¼ tsp salt
- ½ cup (100g) granulated sugar
- ⅓ cup (80ml) vegetable oil
- ⅓ cup (80ml) almond milk (or any plant-based milk)
- 1 tsp vanilla extract
- ½ cup (90g) vegan chocolate chips (optional)

Instructions:
1. Preheat the Air Fryer to 175°C (350°F).
2. In a large mixing bowl, whisk together the flour, cocoa powder, baking powder, and salt.
3. In another bowl, mix together the sugar, vegetable oil, almond milk, and vanilla extract until well combined.
4. Pour the wet ingredients into the dry ingredients and mix until just combined.
5. Fold in the vegan chocolate chips, if using.
6. Grease a square baking pan that fits inside the Air Fryer basket.
7. Pour the batter into the prepared baking pan and spread it evenly.
8. Place the baking pan in the Air Fryer basket.
9. Air fry at 175°C (350°F) for 25 minutes or until a toothpick inserted into the center comes out with a few moist crumbs.
10. Once baked, remove the brownies from the Air Fryer and let them cool completely in the pan.
11. Once cooled, slice the brownies into squares and serve.
12. Enjoy these rich and fudgy vegan brownies as a delicious dessert or snack!

Nutritional Info: Calories: 200 | Fat: 10g | Carbs: 27g | Protein: 2g

Air Fryer Function Used: Baking at 175°C (350°F)

Air Fryer Gluten-Free Lemon Bars

Prep: 20 mins | Cook: 35 mins | Makes: 9 bars

Ingredients:

- 1 cup (120g) gluten-free all-purpose flour
- ¼ cup (50g) granulated sugar
- ½ cup (115g) vegan butter, softened
- 2 tbsp powdered sugar (for dusting)
- 2 large lemons (zest and juice)
- 1 cup (200g) granulated sugar
- 2 tbsp gluten-free all-purpose flour
- 4 tbsp cornstarch
- 4 flax eggs (4 tbsp ground flaxseed + 12 tbsp water)
- Powdered sugar (for dusting)

Instructions:

1. Preheat the Air Fryer to 160°C (320°F).
2. In a mixing bowl, combine the gluten-free flour, ¼ cup granulated sugar, and softened vegan butter. Mix until crumbly.
3. Press the mixture into the bottom of a greased square baking pan that fits inside the Air Fryer basket.
4. Bake the crust in the Air Fryer for 10 minutes.
5. While the crust is baking, prepare the lemon filling. In a separate mixing bowl, whisk together the lemon zest, lemon juice, 1 cup granulated sugar, 2 tablespoons of gluten-free flour, and cornstarch until smooth.
6. Add the flax eggs to the lemon mixture and whisk until well combined.
7. Pour the lemon filling over the baked crust and spread it evenly.
8. Return the baking pan to the Air Fryer and bake for an additional 25 minutes or until the filling is set.
9. Once baked, remove the lemon bars from the Air Fryer and let them cool in the pan.
10. Once cooled, dust the top of the lemon bars with powdered sugar.
11. Slice into squares and serve these tangy gluten-free lemon bars as a delightful treat!

Nutritional Info: Calories: 180 | Fat: 8g | Carbs: 26g | Protein: 2g

Air Fryer Function Used: Baking at 160°C (320°F)

Air Fryer Vegan Apple Cake

Prep: 20 mins | Cook: 35 mins | Serves: 8-10

Ingredients:

- 2 cups (250g) all-purpose flour
- 1 tsp baking powder
- 1 tsp baking soda
- 1 tsp ground cinnamon
- ½ tsp ground nutmeg
- ½ tsp salt
- ½ cup (120ml) vegetable oil
- 1 cup (200g) granulated sugar
- 2 flax eggs (2 tbsp ground flaxseed + 6 tbsp water)
- 1 tsp vanilla extract
- 2 cups (200g) diced apples
- ½ cup (60g) chopped walnuts or pecans (optional)

Instructions:

1. Preheat your Air Fryer to 160°C (320°F).
2. In a large mixing bowl, whisk together the all-purpose flour, baking powder, baking soda, cinnamon, nutmeg, and salt.
3. In another bowl, prepare the flax eggs by mixing together ground flaxseed and water. Let it sit for 5 minutes to thicken.
4. Add the vegetable oil, granulated sugar, flax eggs, and vanilla extract to the dry ingredients. Mix until well combined.
5. Fold in the diced apples and chopped nuts if using until evenly distributed.
6. Grease and line a round cake pan that fits inside the Air Fryer basket.
7. Pour the batter into the prepared cake pan and spread it out evenly.
8. Place the cake pan in the Air Fryer basket and bake at 160°C (320°F) for about 30-35 minutes or until a toothpick inserted into the center comes out clean.
9. Once baked, remove the apple cake from the Air Fryer and let it cool in the pan for a few minutes.
10. Transfer the cake to a wire rack to cool completely before slicing and serving.
11. Enjoy this moist and flavorful vegan apple cake as a delicious dessert or snack!

Nutritional Info: Calories: 220 | Fat: 10g | Carbs: 30g | Protein: 3g

Air Fryer Function Used: Baking at 160°C (320°F)

Air Fryer Gluten-Free Pineapple Upside-Down Cake

Prep: 20 mins | Cook: 35 mins | Serves: 8-10

Ingredients:

- 1 can (20 oz) pineapple slices in juice, drained
- ½ cup (115g) unsalted butter, melted
- ¾ cup (150g) brown sugar
- 1 ½ cups (180g) gluten-free all-purpose flour
- 1 tsp baking powder
- ½ tsp baking soda
- ¼ tsp salt
- ½ cup (120ml) buttermilk or yogurt (dairy-free if needed)
- 2 large eggs
- 1 tsp vanilla extract
- Maraschino cherries for garnish (optional)

Instructions:

1. Preheat your Air Fryer to 160°C (320°F).
2. In a bowl, mix melted butter and brown sugar until well combined. Spread this mixture evenly in the bottom of a greased round cake pan that fits inside the Air Fryer basket.
3. Arrange pineapple slices over the brown sugar mixture in the cake pan. Place a cherry in the center of each pineapple slice if using.
4. In a separate bowl, whisk together the gluten-free flour, baking powder, baking soda, and salt.
5. In another bowl, whisk together the buttermilk or yogurt, eggs, and vanilla extract until well combined.
6. Gradually add the dry ingredients to the wet ingredients, stirring until just combined.
7. Pour the batter over the pineapple slices in the cake pan, spreading it out evenly.
8. Place the cake pan in the Air Fryer basket and bake at 160°C (320°F) for about 30-35 minutes or until a toothpick inserted into the center comes out clean.
9. Once baked, remove the pineapple upside-down cake from the Air Fryer and let it cool in the pan for a few minutes.
10. Carefully invert the cake onto a serving plate. Allow it to cool slightly before slicing and serving.
11. Enjoy this irresistible gluten-free pineapple upside-down cake as a delightful dessert!

Nutritional Info: Calories: 240 | Fat: 9g | Carbs: 38g | Protein: 3g

Air Fryer Vegan Red Velvet Cake

Prep: 20 mins | Cook: 30 mins | Serves: 8-10

Ingredients:

- 1 ½ cups (180g) all-purpose flour
- 1 cup (200g) granulated sugar
- 2 tbsp unsweetened cocoa powder
- 1 tsp baking soda
- ½ tsp salt
- 1 cup (240ml) almond milk (or any plant-based milk)
- ½ cup (120ml) vegetable oil
- 1 tbsp apple cider vinegar
- 1 tsp vanilla extract
- 2 tbsp red food coloring (or beetroot powder for natural coloring)

Instructions:

1. Preheat your Air Fryer to 160°C (320°F).
2. In a large mixing bowl, sift together the all-purpose flour, sugar, cocoa powder, baking soda, and salt.
3. In another bowl, whisk together the almond milk, vegetable oil, apple cider vinegar, vanilla extract, and red food coloring until well combined.
4. Gradually add the wet ingredients to the dry ingredients, stirring until smooth and well combined.
5. Grease and line a round cake pan that fits inside the Air Fryer basket.
6. Pour the batter into the prepared cake pan and spread it out evenly.
7. Place the cake pan in the Air Fryer basket and bake at 160°C (320°F) for about 25-30 minutes or until a toothpick inserted into the center comes out clean.
8. Once baked, remove the red velvet cake from the Air Fryer and let it cool in the pan for 10 minutes.
9. Carefully transfer the cake to a wire rack to cool completely before frosting.
10. Frost the cooled cake with your favorite vegan cream cheese frosting or any desired frosting.
11. Slice and serve this delicious vegan red velvet cake as a decadent dessert for any occasion!

Nutritional Info: Calories: 220 | Fat: 10g | Carbs: 30g | Protein: 2g

Air Fryer Function Used: Baking at 160°C (320°F)

Air Fryer Gluten-Free Blueberry Muffins

Prep: 15 mins | Cook: 20 mins | Serves: 8-10

Ingredients:

- 1 ½ cups (180g) gluten-free all-purpose flour
- ½ cup (100g) granulated sugar
- 2 tsp baking powder
- ½ tsp baking soda
- ¼ tsp salt
- ½ cup (120ml) almond milk (or any plant-based milk)
- ⅓ cup (80ml) vegetable oil
- 1 tsp vanilla extract
- 1 flax egg (1 tbsp ground flaxseed + 3 tbsp water)
- 1 cup (150g) fresh blueberries

1. *Instructions:*

1. Preheat your Air Fryer to 180°C (350°F).
2. In a large mixing bowl, sift together the gluten-free flour, sugar, baking powder, baking soda, and salt.
3. In another bowl, prepare the flax egg by mixing together ground flaxseed and water. Let it sit for 5 minutes to thicken.
4. Add the almond milk, vegetable oil, vanilla extract, and prepared flax egg to the dry ingredients. Mix until well combined.
5. Gently fold in the fresh blueberries until evenly distributed.
6. Line muffin cups with paper liners or lightly grease them.
7. Spoon the muffin batter into the prepared muffin cups, filling each about two-thirds full.
8. Place the muffin tin in the Air Fryer basket, ensuring there is space between each muffin.
9. Air fry at 180°C (350°F) for about 18-20 minutes or until the muffins are golden brown and a toothpick inserted into the center comes out clean.
10. Once baked, remove the muffins from the Air Fryer and let them cool in the muffin tin for a few minutes.
11. Transfer the muffins to a wire rack to cool completely before serving.

12. Enjoy these delightful gluten-free blueberry muffins as a tasty breakfast or snack option!

Nutritional Info: Calories: 180 | Fat: 8g | Carbs: 26g | Protein: 2g

Air Fryer Function Used: Baking at 180°C (350°F)

Air Fryer Vegan Coconut Cake

Prep: 20 mins | Cook: 30 mins | Serves: 8-10

Ingredients:
- 1 ½ cups (180g) all-purpose flour
- 1 cup (200g) granulated sugar
- 1 tsp baking powder
- ½ tsp baking soda
- ¼ tsp salt
- 1 cup (240ml) coconut milk
- ½ cup (120ml) vegetable oil
- 1 tsp vanilla extract
- 1 tbsp apple cider vinegar
- ½ cup (40g) shredded coconut, plus extra for garnish

Instructions:
1. Preheat your Air Fryer to 160°C (320°F).
2. In a large mixing bowl, sift together the all-purpose flour, sugar, baking powder, baking soda, and salt.
3. In another bowl, whisk together the coconut milk, vegetable oil, vanilla extract, and apple cider vinegar until well combined.
4. Gradually add the wet ingredients to the dry ingredients, stirring until smooth and well combined.
5. Fold in the shredded coconut until evenly distributed.
6. Grease and line a round cake pan that fits inside the Air Fryer basket.
7. Pour the batter into the prepared cake pan and spread it out evenly.
8. Place the cake pan in the Air Fryer basket and bake at 160°C (320°F) for about 25-30 minutes or until a toothpick inserted into the center comes out clean.

9. Once baked, remove the coconut cake from the Air Fryer and let it cool in the pan for a few minutes.
10. Carefully transfer the cake to a wire rack to cool completely before frosting.
11. Garnish the cooled cake with additional shredded coconut if desired.
12. Slice and serve this delicious vegan coconut cake as a delightful dessert or snack!

Nutritional Info: Calories: 220 | Fat: 10g | Carbs: 30g | Protein: 2g

Air Fryer Function Used: Baking at 160°C (320°F)

CHAPTER TEN: FROSTINGS, FILLINGS, AND TOPPINGS

Buttercream Frosting

Prep: 10 mins | Cook: 0 mins | Makes: Enough for 1 cake

Ingredients:
- 1 cup (226g) unsalted butter, softened
- 4 cups (500g) icing sugar (UK: powdered sugar)
- 2 tsp vanilla extract
- 2-4 tbsp milk or heavy cream
- Pinch of salt

Instructions:
1. In a mixing bowl, beat the softened butter using an electric mixer until creamy and smooth.
2. Gradually add the icing sugar, about 1 cup at a time, mixing well after each addition until fully incorporated.
3. Add the vanilla extract and a pinch of salt, and continue to beat the mixture until light and fluffy.
4. If the frosting is too thick, gradually add milk or heavy cream, 1 tablespoon at a time, until desired consistency is reached. If it's too thin, add more icing sugar.
5. Once the frosting reaches the desired consistency, it's ready to use. Spread or pipe onto cooled cakes or cupcakes as desired.

Nutritional Info: Calories: 140 | Fat: 7g | Carbs: 20g | Protein: 0g

Air Fryer Function Used: Mixing with Electric Mixer

Cream Cheese Frosting

Prep: 10 mins | Cook: 0 mins | Makes: Enough for 1 cake

Ingredients:
- 1/2 cup (115g) unsalted butter, softened
- 8 oz (225g) cream cheese, softened
- 4 cups (500g) icing sugar (UK: powdered sugar)
- 1 tsp vanilla extract

Instructions:
1. In a mixing bowl, beat the softened butter and cream cheese together until smooth and creamy.
2. Gradually add the icing sugar, about 1 cup at a time, mixing well after each addition until fully incorporated.
3. Add the vanilla extract and continue to beat the mixture until light and fluffy.
4. If the frosting is too thick, you can add a little milk or cream to thin it out, but be careful not to make it too runny.
5. Once the frosting is ready, use it to frost cakes, cupcakes, or any other baked treats as desired.

Nutritional Info: Calories: 180 | Fat: 9g | Carbs: 25g | Protein: 1g

Air Fryer Function Used: Mixing with Electric Mixer

Decadent Chocolate Ganache

Prep: 5 mins | Cook: 5 mins | Makes: Enough for 1 cake

Ingredients:

- 8 oz (225g) good-quality dark chocolate, chopped
- 1 cup (240ml) heavy cream
- 2 tbsp unsalted butter, cubed
- 1 tsp vanilla extract

Instructions:

1. Place the chopped chocolate in a heatproof bowl.
2. In a saucepan, heat the heavy cream over medium heat until it just begins to simmer. Remove from heat immediately.
3. Pour the hot cream over the chopped chocolate and let it sit for a minute to soften the chocolate.
4. Gently stir the mixture until the chocolate is completely melted and the ganache is smooth and glossy.
5. Add the cubed butter and vanilla extract, and stir until the butter is melted and fully incorporated into the ganache.
6. Let the ganache cool for a few minutes before using it to glaze cakes or drizzle over desserts.

Nutritional Info: Calories: 150 | Fat: 15g | Carbs: 7g | Protein: 1g

Air Fryer Function Used: Melting in Saucepan

Caramel Sauce

Prep: 5 mins | Cook: 10 mins | Makes: About 1 cup

Ingredients:
- 1 cup (200g) granulated sugar
- 6 tbsp (85g) unsalted butter, cut into pieces
- 1/2 cup (120ml) heavy cream
- 1 tsp vanilla extract
- Pinch of salt

Instructions:
1. Heat the granulated sugar in a saucepan over medium heat, stirring constantly with a heatproof spatula or wooden spoon.
2. As the sugar melts, it will clump together, but continue stirring until it completely liquefies and turns into a deep amber color.
3. Once the sugar is fully melted and amber in color, immediately add the butter, stirring vigorously until it is completely melted and combined with the sugar.
4. Slowly pour in the heavy cream while stirring constantly. Be careful as the mixture will bubble up.
5. Continue to cook and stir the caramel sauce for another 1-2 minutes until smooth and thickened.
6. Remove the saucepan from the heat and stir in the vanilla extract and a pinch of salt.
7. Let the caramel sauce cool slightly before using. It will thicken as it cools.

Nutritional Info: Calories: 120 | Fat: 8g | Carbs: 15g | Protein: 0g

Air Fryer Function Used: Cooking on Stovetop

Fruit Compote

Prep: 5 mins | Cook: 15 mins | Makes: About 2 cups

Ingredients:
- 2 cups (300g) mixed berries (such as strawberries, blueberries, raspberries)
- 1/4 cup (50g) granulated sugar
- 2 tbsp water
- 1 tsp lemon juice
- 1/2 tsp vanilla extract

Instructions:
1. In a saucepan, combine the mixed berries, granulated sugar, water, lemon juice, and vanilla extract.
2. Cook over medium heat, stirring occasionally, until the berries begin to break down and the mixture thickens slightly, about 10-15 minutes.
3. Once the fruit compote reaches your desired consistency, remove it from the heat and let it cool slightly before serving.
4. You can store any leftovers in an airtight container in the refrigerator for up to one week.

Nutritional Info: Calories: 40 | Fat: 0g | Carbs: 10g | Protein: 0g

Air Fryer Function Used: Cooking on Stovetop

Whipped Cream

Prep: 5 mins | Cook: 0 mins | Makes: Enough for 1 cake

Ingredients:
- 1 cup (240ml) heavy cream
- 2 tbsp powdered sugar (UK: icing sugar)
- 1 tsp vanilla extract

Instructions:
1. In a large mixing bowl, combine the heavy cream, powdered sugar, and vanilla extract.
2. Using a hand mixer or stand mixer, beat the mixture on medium-high speed until stiff peaks form. Be careful not to overbeat, or it will turn into butter.
3. Once the whipped cream reaches the desired consistency, use it immediately to top cakes, pies, or other desserts.

Nutritional Info: Calories: 50 | Fat: 5g | Carbs: 2g | Protein: 0g

Air Fryer Function Used: Mixing with Electric Mixer

Meringue Frosting

Prep: 15 mins | Cook: 2 hours | Makes: Enough for 1 cake

Ingredients:
- 4 large egg whites
- 1 cup (200g) granulated sugar
- 1/4 tsp cream of tartar
- 1 tsp vanilla extract

Instructions:

1. In a heatproof mixing bowl, combine the egg whites, granulated sugar, and cream of tartar.
2. Place the bowl over a pot of simmering water, making sure the bottom of the bowl doesn't touch the water.
3. Whisk constantly until the sugar is completely dissolved and the mixture reaches 160°F (71°C) on a candy thermometer, about 2-3 minutes.
4. Remove the bowl from the heat and transfer it to a stand mixer fitted with the whisk attachment.
5. Beat the mixture on high speed until stiff, glossy peaks form, and the meringue has cooled to room temperature, about 5-7 minutes.
6. Add the vanilla extract and continue to beat for another minute until fully incorporated.
7. Use the meringue frosting immediately to frost cakes or pies. It can also be toasted with a kitchen torch for a beautiful finish.

Nutritional Info: Calories: 25 | Fat: 0g | Carbs: 6g | Protein: 1g

Air Fryer Function Used: Whisking on Stand Mixer

Nut Crumble Topping

Prep: 5 mins | Cook: 15 mins | Makes: Enough for 1 cake

Ingredients:

- 1/2 cup (60g) all-purpose flour (UK: plain flour)
- 1/4 cup (50g) granulated sugar
- 1/4 cup (30g) chopped nuts (such as almonds, pecans, or walnuts)
- 1/4 cup (60g) unsalted butter, cold and cubed

Instructions:

1. In a mixing bowl, combine the all-purpose flour, granulated sugar, and chopped nuts.
2. Add the cold, cubed butter to the bowl and use your fingertips to rub it into the flour mixture until it resembles coarse crumbs.
3. Spread the crumble topping evenly over the cake batter before baking.
4. Bake the cake according to the recipe instructions, or until the topping is golden brown and crispy.

5. Let the cake cool slightly before serving. The nut crumble topping adds a delightful crunch to your baked goods.

Nutritional Info: Calories: 80 | Fat: 5g | Carbs: 8g | Protein: 1g

Air Fryer Function Used: Air Frying

Streusel Topping

Prep: 10 mins | Cook: 15 mins | Makes: Enough for 1 cake

Ingredients:
- 1/2 cup (65g) all-purpose flour (UK: plain flour)
- 1/4 cup (50g) packed brown sugar
- 1/4 cup (30g) rolled oats
- 1/4 tsp ground cinnamon
- Pinch of salt
- 1/4 cup (60g) unsalted butter, cold and cubed

Instructions:
1. In a mixing bowl, combine the all-purpose flour, brown sugar, rolled oats, ground cinnamon, and salt.
2. Add the cold, cubed butter to the bowl and use your fingertips to rub it into the flour mixture until it resembles coarse crumbs.
3. Sprinkle the streusel topping evenly over the cake batter before baking.
4. Bake the cake according to the recipe instructions, or until the topping is golden brown and crispy.
5. Allow the cake to cool slightly before serving. The streusel topping adds a deliciously sweet and crunchy layer to your baked treats.

Nutritional Info: Calories: 90 | Fat: 5g | Carbs: 12g | Protein: 1g

Air Fryer Function Used: Air frying

Glaze Recipes

Prep: 5 mins | Cook: 0 mins | Makes: Enough for 1 cake

Ingredients:

- For Vanilla Glaze:
- 1 cup (120g) powdered sugar (UK: icing sugar)
- 1-2 tbsp milk or water
- 1/2 tsp vanilla extract
- For Chocolate Glaze:
- 1 cup (120g) powdered sugar (UK: icing sugar)
- 2 tbsp unsweetened cocoa powder
- 2-3 tbsp milk or water
- 1/2 tsp vanilla extract

Instructions:

1. For Vanilla Glaze:
   a. In a mixing bowl, whisk together the powdered sugar, milk or water, and vanilla extract until smooth and pourable. Adjust the consistency by adding more milk or powdered sugar as needed.
   b. Drizzle the vanilla glaze over cooled cakes or pastries using a spoon or piping bag.
2. For Chocolate Glaze:
   c. In a mixing bowl, sift together the powdered sugar and cocoa powder to remove any lumps.
   d. Stir in the milk or water and vanilla extract until smooth and glossy. Adjust the consistency with additional milk or powdered sugar if necessary.
   e. Drizzle the chocolate glaze over cooled cakes or pastries using a spoon or piping bag.
3. Allow the glaze to set for a few minutes before serving. Enjoy the glossy finish it adds to your baked goods!

Nutritional Info: Vanilla Glaze: Calories: 40 | Fat: 0g | Carbs: 10g | Protein: 0g

Chocolate Glaze: Calories: 45 | Fat: 0.5g | Carbs: 10g | Protein: 0.5g

Air Fryer Function Used: Mixing in bowl

Chocolate Buttercream

Prep: 10 mins | Cook: 0 mins | Makes: Enough for 1 cake

Ingredients:
- 1 cup (225g) unsalted butter, softened
- 2 1/2 cups (300g) powdered sugar (UK: icing sugar)
- 1/2 cup (50g) unsweetened cocoa powder
- 2-3 tbsp milk or cream
- 1 tsp vanilla extract
- Pinch of salt

Instructions:
1. In a large mixing bowl, beat the softened butter until creamy and smooth.
2. Gradually add the powdered sugar and cocoa powder, beating on low speed until combined.
3. Add the milk or cream, vanilla extract, and a pinch of salt. Increase the speed to medium-high and beat until the frosting is light and fluffy.
4. If the frosting is too thick, add more milk or cream, a tablespoon at a time, until the desired consistency is reached.
5. Use the chocolate buttercream to frost cooled cakes or cupcakes, spreading it evenly over the surface with a spatula or piping it onto desserts with a piping bag.

Nutritional Info: Calories: 160 | Fat: 10g | Carbs: 19g | Protein: 0g

Air Fryer Function Used: Mixing with Electric Mixer

Peanut Butter Frosting

Prep: 10 mins | Cook: 0 mins | Makes: Enough for 1 cake

Ingredients:
- 1/2 cup (115g) unsalted butter, softened
- 1 cup (250g) creamy peanut butter
- 2 cups (240g) powdered sugar (UK: icing sugar)
- 2-3 tbsp milk or cream
- 1 tsp vanilla extract
- Pinch of salt

Instructions:
1. In a large mixing bowl, cream together the softened butter and creamy peanut butter until smooth.
2. Gradually add the powdered sugar, beating on low speed until well combined.
3. Add the milk or cream, vanilla extract, and a pinch of salt. Beat on medium-high speed until the frosting is light and fluffy.
4. If the frosting is too thick, add more milk or cream, a tablespoon at a time, until desired consistency is reached.
5. Use the peanut butter frosting to frost cooled cakes or cupcakes, spreading it evenly over the surface with a spatula or piping it onto desserts with a piping bag.

Nutritional Info: Calories: 180 | Fat: 12g | Carbs: 16g | Protein: 4g

Air Fryer Function Used: Mixing with Electric Mixer

Dulce de Leche Filling

Prep: 5 mins | Cook: 1 hour | Makes: Enough for 1 cake

Ingredients:
- 1 (14 oz) can sweetened condensed milk

Instructions:
1. Pour the sweetened condensed milk into a heatproof container or jar.
2. Seal the container tightly with a lid.
3. Place the sealed container in the air fryer basket.
4. Cook at 176°C (350°F) for 60 minutes, shaking the container every 20 minutes to prevent burning.
5. Once the cooking time is complete, carefully remove the container from the air fryer and let it cool completely before using the dulce de leche as a filling for cakes or other desserts.

Nutritional Info: Calories: 60 (per tablespoon) | Fat: 2g | Carbs: 10g | Protein: 1g

Air Fryer Function Used: Slow cook

Marshmallow Fluff Frosting

Prep: 5 mins | Cook: 0 mins | Makes: Enough for 1 cake

Ingredients:
- 1 cup (200g) granulated sugar
- 1/2 cup (120ml) light corn syrup
- 1/4 cup (60ml) water
- 4 large egg whites, at room temperature
- 1/4 tsp cream of tartar
- 1 tsp vanilla extract
- Pinch of salt

Instructions:

1. In a saucepan, combine the granulated sugar, corn syrup, and water. Cook over medium heat, stirring occasionally, until the sugar dissolves and the mixture reaches 240°F (115°C) on a candy thermometer.
2. While the sugar syrup is cooking, beat the egg whites and cream of tartar in a clean, dry mixing bowl until soft peaks form.
3. Once the sugar syrup reaches the correct temperature, slowly pour it into the beaten egg whites while continuing to beat on high speed.
4. Continue beating until the mixture becomes thick and glossy, about 5-7 minutes.
5. Add the vanilla extract and a pinch of salt, and beat for an additional minute until well combined.
6. Use the marshmallow fluff frosting immediately to frost cakes or cupcakes, spreading it evenly over the surface with a spatula or piping it onto desserts with a piping bag.

Nutritional Info: Calories: 60 | Fat: 0g | Carbs: 16g | Protein: 1g

Air Fryer Function Used: Mixing with Electric Mixer

Swiss Meringue Buttercream

Prep: 20 mins | Cook: 0 mins | Makes: Enough for 1 cake

Ingredients:

- 4 large egg whites
- 1 cup (200g) granulated sugar
- 1 1/2 cups (340g) unsalted butter, softened
- 1 tsp vanilla extract
- Pinch of salt

Instructions:

1. In a heatproof mixing bowl, whisk together the egg whites and granulated sugar.
2. Place the bowl over a saucepan of simmering water (double boiler) and whisk constantly until the sugar has dissolved and the mixture reaches 160°F (70°C) on a candy thermometer.
3. Remove the bowl from the heat and transfer it to a stand mixer fitted with the whisk attachment.

4. Beat the egg white mixture on high speed until stiff peaks form and the bowl is cool to the touch, about 10-15 minutes.
5. Gradually add the softened butter, a few tablespoons at a time, while continuing to beat on medium-high speed.
6. Once all the butter has been incorporated, add the vanilla extract and a pinch of salt. Beat for an additional 2-3 minutes until the frosting is smooth and creamy.
7. Use the Swiss meringue buttercream immediately to frost cakes or cupcakes, spreading it evenly over the surface with a spatula or piping it onto desserts with a piping bag.

Nutritional Info: Calories: 180 | Fat: 18g | Carbs: 6g | Protein: 1g

Air Fryer Function Used: Mixing with Electric Mixer

Fruit Curd Fillings

Prep: 10 mins | Cook: 10 mins | Makes: Enough for 1 cake

Ingredients:
- 1/2 cup (100g) granulated sugar
- Zest of 1 lemon or orange
- 1/2 cup (120ml) fresh lemon or orange juice
- 3 large eggs
- 1/4 cup (60g) unsalted butter, cubed

Instructions:
1. In a saucepan, whisk together the granulated sugar, lemon or orange zest, lemon or orange juice, and eggs until well combined.
2. Place the saucepan over medium heat and cook, stirring constantly, until the mixture thickens and coats the back of a spoon, about 5-7 minutes.
3. Remove the saucepan from the heat and whisk in the cubed unsalted butter until smooth and well combined.
4. Strain the fruit curd through a fine-mesh sieve to remove any lumps or zest.
5. Transfer the fruit curd to a clean jar or container and let it cool to room temperature before using it as a filling for cakes or other desserts.

Nutritional Info: Calories: 80 | Fat: 5g | Carbs: 8g | Protein: 2g

Air Fryer Function Used: Cooking on Stovetop

Conclusion

As we reach the end of our journey into the world of air fryer cake baking, I hope you've gained not only a wealth of knowledge, but also a sense of excitement and confidence. What may have once seemed like an unconventional or even implausible idea – baking delicious cakes in a compact air fryer – has been revealed as an innovative and rewarding technique.

Throughout this book, we've explored the unique benefits of air fryer baking, from energy efficiency and precise temperature control, to faster bake times and consistent, even results. We've learned how to select the ideal air fryer for your baking needs, mastered essential preheating methods, and discovered ways to adapt traditional cake recipes for air frying success.

But beyond just the technical know-how, I hope I've been able to impart some of the sheer joy and creativity that air fryer cake baking can bring. This unconventional approach opens up a world of possibilities, allowing you to experiment with flavors, textures, and decorative designs in a way that feels fresh and exciting.

I can't even begin to count how many times I've been amazed by the impressive cakes emerging from my little air fryer – towering layers with a tender crumb, intricately sculpted Bundts with incredible detail, and rich, fudgy creations that look (and taste) like they came straight from a professional bakery. And each time, I'm reminded of why I fell in love with this unique baking method in the first place.

Watching that very first air fryer cake rise up perfectly domed, filling my kitchen with an aroma that made my mouth water, I knew I had stumbled onto something special. As I anxiously pulled it from the air fryer basket, I couldn't believe the beautiful golden crust and gravity-defying height it had achieved in such a compact space. That first slice revealed an interior that was feather-light yet incredibly moist, with a delicate crumb that seemed to melt on my tongue. In that moment, I was utterly sold on air fryer baking.

From there, my curiosity only continued to grow as I experimented with different recipes, flavors, and techniques. Classics like moist yellow cake and decadent chocolate transferred beautifully to the air fryer. More complex creations, from luscious red velvet bundt cakes to coconut-layered pineapple delights, emerged just as impressive. I even started inventing my own custom cakes designed specifically for air frying, combining flavors and indulgent mix-ins in delightfully unique ways.

With every creation that came out of that marvelous little oven, I felt more and more like I'd unlocked a secret baking superpower. What had once been a hassle – firing up my conventional oven, struggling with uneven baking, or wrestling with scorching hot pans – became an absolute joy thanks to the air fryer's ease and consistent results. Baking was suddenly an effortless indulgence that I could enjoy any day of the week.

Of course, with that new passion came a flurry of requests from friends and family to bake up air-fried treats for gatherings and celebrations. I was more than happy to oblige, receiving wide-eyed wonder and utter delight as I unveiled each creation waiting for them in my air fryer. From birthday cakes festooned with sprinkles to cream-filled strawberry cupcakes to eye-catching mirror-glazed Bundt crowns, people were amazed that such gorgeous desserts could come from such a compact and unassuming appliance on my countertop.

But their amazement was always short-lived once they took their first bite and experienced the sheer perfection made possible by air fryer baking. That's when the real magic became clear — no matter how implausible it may have seemed initially, these air-fried cakes delivered bakery-caliber taste and texture unlike anything most had experienced from a home oven.

I hope that somewhere within these pages, you've had your own "aha!" moment that sparked your passion for air fryer desserts. Perhaps it was reading about adapting grandma's classic pound cake into a tall, buttery Bundt with a crackling sugary crust. Or maybe envisioning those chocolate cupcakes with a molten lava center that can be yours in under 30 minutes of air fryer time. Whenever that spark of inspiration strikes, I want you to feel empowered to dive in and create without hesitation or doubt.

Remember, at its core, baking is about combining simple ingredients in specific ratios and environments to manifest something utterly transcendent and magical. By having the wits to look beyond conventional oven restrictions, you open yourself up to infinite possibilities in the realm of desserts. Who's to say an air fryer can't be the baking vessel for YOUR edible masterpiece?

So keep experimenting, keep playing with flavors and frostings, and keep that beautiful baking spirit alive. Whether you're whipping up a casual weekend tea cake or an elaborately decorated showstopper, let your air fryer be the secret weapon that elevates your creations to new heights of deliciousness. You've got this!

Most of all, don't forget to pause and savor the sheer enjoyment and pride that comes from baking your own air-fried desserts from scratch. With each addictive aroma wafting from that marvelous appliance and each delightfully moist, decadent bite, you'll experience the undeniable magic and satisfaction that can only come from getting a little hands-on in the kitchen.

Here's to many more delicious adventures in air fryer baking that await! I'll be first in line with forks at the ready to try whatever sweet masterpiece emerges from YOUR miraculous little oven. Happy baking!